P9-APP-997

EARLY CHILDHOOD EDUCATION SERIES
Sharon Ryan, Editor

(continued)

Starting with Their Strengths

Using the Project Approach in Early Childhood Special Education

Deborah C. Lickey
Denise J. Powers

Foreword by Lesley Koplow

Teachers College, Columbia University
New York and London

Published by Teachers College Press, 1234 Amsterdam Avenue, New York, NY 10027

Library of Congress Cataloging-in-Publication Data

Lickey, Deborah C.
  Starting with their strengths : using the project approach in early childhood special education / Deborah Lickey, Denise Powers ; foreword by Lesley Koplow.
      p. cm. -- (Early childhood education series)
  Includes bibliographical references and index.
  ISBN 978-0-8077-5234-0 (pbk. : alk. paper) -- ISBN 978-0-8077-5235-7 (hardcover : alk. paper)
  1. Children with disabilities--Education (Early childhood)--United States. 2. Special education--United States. 3. Project method in teaching. I. Powers, Denise J. II. Title.
  LC4019.3.L54 2011
  371.90973--dc23   *2011017771*

ISBN 978-0-8077-5234-0 (paper)
ISBN 978-0-8077-5235-7 (hardcover)

Printed on acid-free paper
Manufactured in the United States of America

18   17   16   15   14   13   12   11   8   7   6   5   4   3   2   1

Contents

Foreword

Preschool children are too young to be articulate about their learning processes, and they cannot describe the teaching models that will facilitate their feelings of social competence, emotional well-being, and cognitive mastery in the classroom. Fortunately, Deborah Lickey and Denise Powers, the authors of *Starting with Their Strengths*, have written a book that describes all of this seamlessly, using the voices of young children and their teachers along with relevant literature to support their work.

The title of *Starting with Their Strengths* lets readers know that they will be reading about the value of engaging young children through their interests, knowledge base, sense of curiosity, and way of relating to others. As the reader gets further into the book, he or she will discover a classroom model where use of emergent curriculum, strong teacher–child relationships, and innovative peer interaction strategies build a classroom community that works for children with autism as well as typically developing children; for withdrawn children as well as children who act out their distress; and for language-delayed children as well as highly verbal children.

Indeed, *Starting with Their Strengths* advocates the application of emergent curriculum and relationship-based learning in classrooms that include children on the autism spectrum, emotionally fragile children, and children whose language limitations preclude communication through verbal means. The authors clearly view children with special needs as children on a continuum of human development who have more in common with typically developing children than may be apparent. Like Vivian Paley in *The Boy Who Would Be a Helicopter*, Lickey and Power's ability to start with children's strengths and stay with children as they slowly build bridges between their internal worlds and the outside world around them helps children give birth to the development of self and the capacity to appreciate others. The approach advocated in this book brings meaning back to the promise that early childhood educators will be involved with the whole child.

Starting with Their Strengths is the right book at the right time. In an era when concern about the performance of older children often pushes early childhood practice to be developmentally inappropriate and academically pressured, Lickey and Powers bring us back to developmental reality. They remind us of how young children learn, and they draw on the work of giants in the field, including Vygotsky, Paley, and the Reggio Emilia schools, to invent a viable way of teaching young children in the 21st century.

Starting with Their Strengths should be required reading for students of early childhood education, practicing teachers, and those who influence educational policy for our youngest learners. If these methods were the rule instead of the exception, all of our young children, not to mention our teachers and professionals working in special education settings, would benefit.

—Lesley Koplow

Acknowledgments

We have always known in our hearts that children are competent learners who can imagine and think great ideas. We are indebted to Irene Carney and Marty Gravette for creating a learning atmosphere that honors this at Sabot at Stony Point School, in Richmond, Virginia, formally known as The Sabot School. Together at Sabot at Stony Point they have cultivated an environment rich with child-centered theories in education and best practices. At Sabot, children and adults are researchers, collaborators, and co-constructors of learning. This has led to children becoming unabashed imaginers, driven thinkers and learners, and thoughtful problem-solvers, and has helped adults remember how to be unabashed imaginers, driven thinkers and learners, and thoughtful problem-solvers.

We also want to acknowledge the many instructional assistants with whom we have worked over the years, those unsung heroes in education who rarely get the recognition they so richly deserve. These talented women have, over the years, contributed their own special wisdom, energy, talents, and support. Without that support, it would have been impossible for us to stretch our own practice as we have strived to learn more about teaching young children. We, Denise and Debbie, realize that as Sabot staff members, not only did we help each other to raise our children, but we also helped to raise each other even higher as women.

I, Denise, wish to acknowledge my mother, Isobel Kelly, who is bestowed with the gift of blathering and who taught me the art of expressing my ideas. My father, Jack Kelly, modeled perseverance through challenging circumstances and tasks. These two sets of skills—communication and perseverance—along with their reminders to carve some time to breathe and rejuvenate, have served me well while writing.

My husband, Mike, genuinely assured me that I could and should write this book, and he graciously took care of our life as I did. Our three daughters, Hannah, Tess, and Emma, all attended The Sabot School. Throughout the process of writing this book, they continued, now as young women, to appreciate and champion their mom's passionate interest in bringing this project to life. Our dogs, Sam, Hershey, and Jake, faithfully listened as I read aloud what I had typed, often in the wee hours of the morning, and provided as many walks as I needed to clear my mind. Thank you, Mike, Hannah, Tess, Emma, and Charlie, for caring for one another, our beloved dogs, and our home throughout this process. Kudos must go to my sister, Kim, for continuing to remind our female-rich family that we come from a long line of brilliant women. We truly are capable of doing anything!

I must also acknowledge the inspiration I found in the strength of my cousin Diane as she battles cancer. Her thoughts and actions have guaranteed that our family will forever share her passion for keeping us all connected with her children and one another. What a gift for us all.

I, Debbie, would like to begin by thanking my family. So much of my life, and especially my work experience, has been a result of the influence of my family. My mother, Doris Crawford, provided me with a respect and passion for education, a love of literacy, and, of course, the unconditional love and support that only comes from a mother. My father, Jim Crawford, provided me with a clear understanding of being able to do "anything that you put your mind to"; the conviction of following through with what you think is right, no matter the consequences; and a love of learning and nature. These gifts from my parents have served me well throughout my life. My siblings, Doug, Dave, Diane, and Alan, have provided me with the need to think creatively (at times), a sense of humor, unending support and love, and a definite sense of goofiness.

My husband, Mike, a gifted writer himself, taught me the skill of writing when we were both college underclassmen and newlyweds. This knowledge allowed me to surpass what I thought I could accomplish academically, and Mike has continued to share his ideas and love, which have sustained me throughout my adult life. My children, Jake, Danielle, and Hannah, have truly taught me about love itself, and about children's innate love of learning, sense of adventure, and curiosity about the world. My best memories in life will always be the times that I was privy to their wonder as they grew.

Both my kids and my husband have, in their own way, provided support, humor, and encouragement as I have written this book, as they made the dinners, cleaned the house, and bought the groceries.

I also want to thank the many dogs that have provided me with opportunities for walks and the kind of stress relief that comes from their curling up beside me as I write: April, Shiloh, Bucky, and Loki, your love means more than you know.

We wish to acknowledge the talented work of photographer Mark Harley, who used his skills to enhance our photos for this book.

Many thanks to Adee Braun, Marie Ellen Larcada, Shannon Waite, and John Bylander from Teachers College Press, whose infinite patience, knowledge, and wisdom took us through the long and sometimes daunting experience of expressing on paper what has impassioned us as educators.

Using Children's Strengths to Create Invested and Curious Preschool Learners

The idea of project-based learning has recently been given much attention in the early childhood field, and for good reason. Project-based learning is designed to provide children with authentic and developmentally appropriate experiences based on children's own strengths, ideas, and interests. Project-based learning expands children's experiences in the preschool classroom, from teacher-directed plans and curriculum to a more emergent curriculum in which the children are active collaborators with their teachers. Children learn the concepts and skills needed in these early years as a part of the learning process as a whole. This process of learning and teaching is a joyful and enriching experience for all involved.

We have practiced this project-based collaboration of learning for many years in our own classrooms after having been provided the experience of observing teachers using similar strategies in their classrooms in Reggio Emilia, Italy. Oftentimes we have been questioned by other early childhood teachers about the actual day-in and day-out process of such learning, such as how to make plans around the project, how to determine what makes a project viable, and how to determine which interests the children will be invested in enough to follow through with activities as they become challenging. We answer these questions by presenting a clear framework for beginning the process of teaching in the project-based manner as we provide theoretical and practical evidence of the efficacy of such an approach.

In this book, we challenge the idea that young children learn best by completing certain activities that have been planned and prepared solely by a teacher who then transmits that information to the children. Our contention is that having many activities to complete does not, in fact, equal learning. We endeavor to ask the question, "Are we writing plans for what we are teaching or for the children's learning?" Is there a difference? You bet there is! Our goal is to offer the reader permission to respect all children, regardless of their developmental abilities, as competent researchers and learners, and to help teachers provide children with authentic learning opportunities that take into account each child's current developmental level. These authentic learning experiences are based on the children's strengths, which include his or her interests, unique intelligences, learning styles, temperament, and skills. Basing learning on strengths validates young children and their capabilities and ideas, which invests the children in learning and leads to self-initiation, socialization, problem-solving, reasoning, and much more (Sandall, Hemmeter, Smith, & McLean, 2005).

Throughout the book, we will refer to strengths-based education. Strengths-based education is based on the philosophy that all children have a basis from which to begin a meaningful and authentic process of discovery and learning. In a strengths-based approach, teachers observe children to learn about the children's own means of learning, their interests in the world, and the natural strengths that children bring to their own development process. Learning about and planning around children's strengths and interests allows teachers to actively engage children so that they become active, engaged participants in their own learning.

In addition to learning the usual standards-based concepts such as shapes, colors, position, and so forth—which, of course, are important and necessary—young children are also capable of:

- Finding out what they are good at
- Finding out what interests and excites them
- Becoming curious learners (which translates into initiative)
- Learning that they have good ideas
- Learning that their opinions matter
- Learning that others can help them further their ideas and plans
- Learning that observing others can give them good ideas
- Learning that they can help others further their ideas
- Learning that they can go to peers to think and talk about ideas
- Learning they can go to teachers to think and talk about ideas
- Learning how to plan, process, and follow through with plans
- Learning how to negotiate with others in order to follow through with plans
- Learning to follow directions in order to help with peers' plans
- Being able to handle new situations
- Learning to follow through with activities (even when they don't want to) in order to achieve something they desire

How do we, as early childhood educators, empower young children with and without disabilities to discover the strengths within themselves? We have, over the past 25 years, studied and been influenced by multiple approaches, researchers, co-workers, and experts in the field of early childhood education. The works and writings of world-renowned pedagogical theorists such as Malaguzzi, Vygotsky, Piaget, Gardner, Greenspan, and Koplow have both informed and validated our strengths-based approach to teaching. The talented and amazing teachers at The Sabot School in Richmond, Virginia, have provided incredible role models and, with their vision, created an opportunity for us to travel to Reggio Emilia, Italy, so that we could study and learn from the teachers and parents involved with the Reggio Emilia schools. The visionaries at these schools have developed an exemplary approach to early childhood learning, and the Reggio Emilia school system has been hailed as among the 10 best in the world.

Having these resources available to us helped us recognize several key components about young children:

- All children have strengths that create a firm foundation for who they can become as learners and as citizens of our world.
- Each of us has many intelligences, or languages, that promote optimal learning and competence, and it is vital to identify those intelligences for children to further develop their strengths. It is, in fact, each adult's responsibility to determine how to engage each child's intelligences, interests, and strengths.
- Just as society would never expect one adult to be able to demonstrate the ability to be an engineer, a teacher, a mechanic, a doctor, a hairstylist, and a police officer all at one time, it is equally unrealistic to expect every child to master every aspect of the curriculum that is offered in our schools. Rather, educators, families, and policymakers need to recognize and respect the individuality of each child's brain and his or her specific learning style. Adults can then teach to the strengths of the child and provide support for areas of curriculum that are more difficult for that particular brain of that particular child.
- Each child, from the beginning of his or her life, is a competent learner who benefits from interaction with adults who will support him or her in the pursuit of what he or she wants and needs to know, rather than an adult who has already decided what and how to teach that child.
- Children must be regulated in their emotions and sensory systems in order to learn, and it is our responsibility as teachers to provide children with the strategies and tools to achieve that self-regulation.

Within this book, we provide evidence-based information about the effectiveness of our approach as well as a thorough guide as to how to go about the process of teaching in this manner.

Chapter 1 begins this journey by providing vignettes that demonstrate how teaching within a strengths-based approach can be exciting and joyful both for each child, when his or her interests and ideas have been respected, and for each teacher, when he or she is able to discover and learn along with their students. Chapters 2 and 3 provide information about getting started with this approach, from observing children in order to assess and determine their strengths and interests, to beginning the process of planning for the children's arrival on the first days of school, and so forth. Chapter 4 emphasizes the benefits of supporting young children in building social and emotional attachments with others at school and encouraging their connections to the environment and materials available for their use.

Chapters 5 and 6 offer the reader evidence-based research, calling for children's active engagement in negotiating the curriculum and learning plans as they emerge with the teacher and therapists. Chapter 5 speaks to setting up the environment and materials in a manner that facilitates the project approach, as the curriculum emerges based on children's interests. Chapter 6 clarifies the planning process in using the project approach, takes the reader through the development of an emergent project, and provides examples of modifying a more traditional themed unit to better reflect the interests and ideas of the children in the class. Chapter 6 offers two lesson plans to reflect these processes of planning.

Chapter 7 brings the strengths-based process full circle by demonstrating the benefits of incorporating strengths-based approaches into the IEP (Individualized Education Plan) process. Finally, Chapter 8 steps back to look at how a strengths-based approach promotes strong relationships that can positively affect not just the students, but their families, teachers, and the wider school community.

In this book, we provide examples of strategies that will offer both new and veteran teachers practical information on using a strengths-based approach in their own classrooms. We also will provide the reader with thorough guidance on how to begin, support, document, and follow through with such an approach. We feel certain that educators, when given the permission to teach from their own interests and strengths and to recognize the same in their students, will find themselves on a joyous adventure in teaching that will revitalize their own sense of wonder about the learning process. The challenges of determining children's strengths and interests and then acting on them to create a mutually satisfying learning experience culminates in a renewal of teachers' own creative energies as they experience daily discoveries with their students.

CHAPTER 1

Imagining the Possibilities of Strengths-Based Learning

Imagine a child with autism exhibiting behaviors typically seen in children with autism, including perseveration (repeating the same behavior or task over and over again) and self-stimulation with increased vocal and physical assaults to others and to himself when attempts were made to calm him. Imagine this child demonstrating other typical behaviors of severe autism disorder, such as screaming at peers, kicking, biting himself and others, pulling his hair, and other self-injurious behaviors, with no means of communication about his fears or feelings.

Now imagine this same child, on his last day of school, attending his school's traditional End-of-Year-Circle, a gathering of students, teachers, and family members for the sharing of closing songs and sentiments. At the end of the very sensory-stimulating ceremony, he is not biting himself or pulling his hair. He is not screaming and covering his ears. He is not flicking objects before his eyes. Rather, as his mother walks him over to say good-bye to Irene, the director of the school, he reaches out and hugs her.

As early childhood educators, we now realize that we cannot respectfully or effectively teach children unless we fully know them. Traditionally, we have focused our understanding of children on their physical, motor, behavioral, and cognitive development. What we better understand today is that the development of each child's emotional, sensory, and social systems creates the pathways for cognitive learning.

This sets for us the seemingly daunting task of attempting to know multiple facets of each individual child through a daily exploration of who that child is at many different levels. Our schools attempt to provide information and activities that are generally developmentally appropriate. What we have come to know is that within each child's many systems of development, varying rates of development can exist. In working with children who have developmental delays we often see a scattering of developmental skills.

For example, children in the autism spectrum might have skills associated with systems (such as learning rote skills, putting together puzzles, and sorting and categorizing) that are on level or even advanced developmentally. However, these same children often are not able to communicate their needs effectively or follow simple directions relating to the barriers that competencies in receptive and expressive language often pose.

5

WESLEY'S STORY

The authors of this book began their strengths-based approach to facilitating the learning of young children with special needs at The Sabot School, in Richmond, Virginia. At The Sabot School, a preschool primarily populated with typically developing peers, the faculty had not had experience with children who were on the more severe end of the autism spectrum. There was the expected uneasiness about whether the school could meet the needs of Wesley, who was a child with severe autism. Fortunately, the teachers were given the gift of an educated and visionary director, Dr. Irene Carney, who not only held a doctorate in Early Childhood Special Education, but who grew up with the experience of having a younger sibling with a severe disability. Irene was calm but clear in her assessment of the situation: Didn't this child have every right to be a part of this school community if his parents chose this environment? Irene pointed out that every child at the school has needs and challenges as well as individual strengths and interests. Wesley and his family were welcomed into the school environment.

The question was asked, "Where do we, as teachers, start with this child?" It was clear from his behaviors that Wesley was in a place of fear and extreme agitation. The question was asked: "How do we help him to feel safe and facilitate his ability to develop self-calming skills with all the stimuli he will be exposed to in a classroom with nine other 2½-year-olds?" The answer came from Irene, whose background included experience with children in the autism spectrum and, more important perhaps, who has a gift for intuitive problem-solving related to children and their needs. Irene suggested a slower start to the day for Wesley, and took on the responsibility of providing that for him. Rather than forcing him to immediately deal with the onslaught of stimuli that he faced upon arrival in his assigned classroom, at the beginning of the day, Irene would take Wesley to an empty room and provide him with sensory experiences, such as proprioceptive feedback in the form of overall body pressure, to aid in his adjustment to the school environment.

Once Irene felt that Wesley seemed regulated enough to handle the adjustment to the classroom, she would return with him. In the classroom the teachers provided Wesley with the necessary supports to help him cope with the environment. Some of these strategies included wrapping him in a small rug and allowing him to come out of this improvised cocoon when he was ready and providing him with a weighted vest to allow for proprioceptive input. Teachers also respected that Wesley needed permission to use materials in a manner that would be meaningful for him, such as allowing him to sift through a small bin of beads rather than expecting him to bead with the class. The teachers gradually became more aware of how to modify materials and activities so that Wesley could interact with them without becoming overstimulated. Teachers were learning about Wesley's needs along with him that year, using Wesley's reactions as a barometer of how successful they were.

There has been a wider recognition among educators of the impact that each child's sensory system has on his or her ability to take in new information, create and maintain social connections, and develop meaningful communication. The sensory system is made up of the five commonly-known senses: touch, taste, smell, hearing, and sight, as well as two other systems that are not as commonly known, but are, ironically, vital to a child's ability: the vestibular sense and the proprioceptive sense. The vestibular sense relates to the senses of equilibrium and of balance, and the proprioceptive sense is related to a receptor found in muscles, tendons, joints, and the inner ear that detects the motion or position of the body. There is a vast body of work that enlightens our understanding of the connection between the sensory systems and development and the role that they play in education. Each child must be capable of regulating him- or herself in order to learn.

Carol Stock Kranowitz (1998) has written for parents (and educators!) about recognizing and coping with the "out of sync child" in their midst, and Pratibha Reebye and Aileen Stalker, in their 2008 book *Understanding Regulation Disorders of Sensory Processing in Children*, guide their readers through understanding how sensory integration typically develops in young children. They emphasize ways to detect when children are experiencing sensory integration dysfunction and offer strategies for supporting these children.

The Sabot staff as a whole began to observe Wesley in the school environment to determine not only his sensory needs and challenges, but also his interests and strengths. What might create opportunities to involve him in the activities of his peers? After some time, teachers realized that Wesley was much happier when given some time in the morning to be outside and play in the sandbox, sifting the sand through his fingers. The staff decided to allow him some time in what might be thought of as perseverative behavior. (Perseverative behaviors can be described as behaviors that are repeated over and over again.) The thought process was to examine this behavior to discover the purpose it served.

One of this book's authors, Denise, had previously taught elementary special education. Irene asked Denise if she would be comfortable accompanying Wesley to the sandbox every morning so he could have time to sift the sand. Because Denise had a bachelor's degree in education with certification in both special and elementary education, as well as 6 years of experience teaching in self-contained special education classrooms, she found herself grappling with the following questions: "How long do we stay here sifting? How will I know when he is finished? Shouldn't I take him in quickly and get his real day started? What if his mother, who works in the upstairs of our building, looks out the window and sees us?"

One day it rained. Actually, it poured. Despite the rain, Wesley wanted to go out to sift in the sand. Denise took an umbrella and she and Wesley walked out to the sand. Wesley repeatedly let the clumps of wet sand fall to the ground as Denise crouched next to him holding the umbrella over his head. He continued to hold the clumps in his field of vision and let them drop to the ground until something caught his attention. It was the drip, drip, dripping of the rain rolling off the umbrella and down Denise's back. Denise questioned the value of sitting in the pouring rain with Wesley as they walked back to the building. Yet, it was not Wesley's mother who was watching them through the window as they sat in the pouring rain; it was Irene. Irene shared how moved she felt watching Denise hold the umbrella over Wesley so that he could sift the sand. On that day, Denise was not convinced that Irene's suggestion to afford Wesley time to sift sand was sound. Yet, when she allowed herself to trust her own knowledge and instincts and to respect Wesley's needs and interests, she soon realized that Irene was right.

Irene found a meaningful way to reach Wesley. She used their time outside, his favorite place to be, and one of his favorite activities, riding in the wagon, as bridges to many other learning opportunities. Irene filled the wagon with sand to entice Wesley to leave the sandbox and engage in another activity with the potential for peer interaction. He would turn his back to anyone interrupting his sifting of the sand while in the sandbox, but while in the wagon (could the handle have given enough space between himself and his peers?) he was able to tolerate children being near him and talking to him, and eventually he was delighted in the vestibular input of being pulled by his peers.

Donna, an extern student from the local university, came to Sabot as a resource for Wesley and our staff. Donna introduced strategies to support Wesley's communication and play. After pulling Wesley for a while, Donna would stop and wait for him to indicate his desire for more pulling. After some time of imitation, Donna began to teach him meaningful communication using his own interests, and he was able to use the sign for more. The other children in the school were interested in this fun activity and gradually began asking to pull Wesley. The staff was thrilled one day to see a typically developing peer pulling Wesley in the wagon, stopping to ask in sign language if Wesley wanted to be pulled more. They were even more thrilled to see Wesley respond with the sign for more! Was this the same child who, a few months ago, could not even cope with being in the room with other children without hurting himself or others?

As the year progressed, the staff continued to explore ways to connect with Wesley and discover who he was. It became clear rather quickly that Wesley was fascinated by light. The teachers had read many different theories and opinions about handling these perseverative behaviors, most of which, at the time, advised extinguishing such behaviors as quickly as possible. Many children in the autism spectrum exhibit such behaviors, which can present as turning lights on and off, flicking objects in line of their eye sight, lining up objects, spinning excessively, and so forth. Although the teachers understood the fact that these behaviors can at times distract the child from other stimuli or learning experiences, questions also arose about what purpose these behaviors filled and how they might be used to aid Wesley in his development.

One bright and beautiful autumn day, the other author of this book, Debbie, was outside in the sandbox with Wesley. They were sifting sand together, and Debbie was feeling pretty excited about the fact that he was allowing her to engage him in increasing circles of reciprocal play, taking turns pouring sand, covering each other's hands, and so forth. As Debbie was pouring sand over Wesley's hand, he looked up from his hand and past her to the trees behind them. Debbie explains her feelings that day: "I watched this child's beautiful face light up, and he looked me directly in the eyes, smiled, and looked at the trees again. I turned to see what had fascinated Wesley to the point that he was making this attempt to share it with me. I saw what had probably been there every day that the sun shone, but which I had overlooked for many years: the almost heavenly beauty of the sun glowing and twinkling through golden, red, and orange leaves of the trees. I looked at Wesley and he looked back at me—who was the teacher now? It was clearly and without doubt a spiritual moment that we shared. At that point it was difficult to see clearly with the tears that blurred my vision, but that was okay. I haven't stopped looking since."

If the act of sifting sand had been seen only as a perseverative behavior to be extinguished, would that connection have been made between Wesley and his teachers that year?

USING STRENGTHS TO PROMOTE DEVELOPMENT

The following year, Wesley appeared to feel more safe and comfortable in the school environment. He was spending less time vocalizing distress, and his self-injurious behaviors had diminished greatly. Yet, he continued to engage in the self-stimulatory behaviors of flicking objects in his field of vision and sitting in the light of the windowsill until redirected. He was beginning to communicate with PECS (Picture Exchange Communication System) and sign language, though he was neither opening nor closing circles of communication with his peers. Circles of communication, a phrase coined by Dr. Stanley Greenspan (Greenspan & Wieder 1998), refers to communication (verbal or nonverbal) in which two active participants respond and interact with one another. For example, a small child points to a cookie while looking at a parent. The parent asks, "Do you want a cookie?" and the child verbalizes or gestures that she does. A circle of communication has been completed. As these interactions expand, the participants open and close additional circles of communication. One of the teachers, Sara, used this self-stimulatory behavior as an opportunity to make a connection between the children in the room and Wesley. The children in the class had noticed Wesley's fascination with bells, so Sara introduced the idea of the children making bells for him to use on their door. This connection helped to make Wesley a more included member of the school community through his stopping and playing in fairly close proximity to the other children, who then felt a sense of investment in making connections with Wesley.

Sara wrote a note to Wesley from the children in her class and posted it on the door to the classroom. It read:

Dear Wesley,
The children have noticed that you have been enjoying our bells so they have made some extra bells for you.

Wesley began to initiate games with his teachers such as horseback rides, bouncing on large therapy balls, and being swung into the air. These strengths and interests were again used to support Wesley in making connections with his peers.

SOCIAL-EMOTIONAL DEVELOPMENT

The development of the social-emotional system is tied to the development of the sensory system. Recently attention to the importance of this system has increased. Dr. Barry Brazelton (1992) has written about the significance of social-emotional development in his book, *Touchpoints*. Other leaders in early childhood development also stress the connection between social-emotional development and learning. Stanley Greenspan (1997) offers that it has been well documented for years that infants learn about their world by using their senses and that through these sensations they develop increasingly complex emotions. What we now know and can apply to learning is the knowledge that each child's sensory system is unique and that his or her experiences and interactions with the world are affected by that sensory system. Those experiences, in turn, affect the child's social-emotional development. Greenspan (1997) tells us that

> in the normal course of events, each sensation, as it is registered by the child, also gives rise to an affect or emotion. It is this *dual coding* of experience that is the key to understanding how emotions organize intellectual capacities and indeed create the sense of self. (p. 18)

Dr. Greenspan developed a guide for social development that he refers to as the six milestones of emotional development. The six milestones build on one another as a developmental ladder and, as a result, "help develop critical cognitive, social, emotional, language and motor skills, as well as a sense of self." (Greenspan & Wieder, 1998, p. 70). These six milestones are as follows:

Milestone 1: Self-Regulation and Interest in the World
Milestone 2: Intimacy
Milestone 3: Two-way Communication
Milestone 4: Complex Communication
Milestone 5: Emotional Ideas
Milestone 6: Emotional Thinking

Dr. Greenspan impresses upon us the importance of taking children through these stages of emotional development, and he provides in-depth information regarding how to aid children as they move through these stages in his book *The Child with Special Needs* (Greenspan & Wieder, 1998). The belief that adults must allow children to move through these stages of development as well as aid them in this process has been a foundation for many of our research and practice with young children.

Experts in the field of early childhood development emphasize the need to recognize the connections between emotional development and development in all other domains of learning. They each verify that a child will best receive information at school when the child is emotionally connected to his or her teachers (adult or peer) and to a nurturing environment and when the child is emotionally invested in the learning (Greenspan & Wieder, 1998; Koplow, 2007; National Research Council Institute of Medicine, 2000; Siegel, 1999). Koplow assures us that "A young child's cognitive and emotional development progress hand in hand. In order for a young child to find meaning in learning experiences, her whole being—including her emotional self—must be involved in the process" (Koplow, 2007, p. 48). Greenspan stresses that, "A program of emotional cuing . . . exploits the role of emotion in normal mental development . . . It appears more effective in fostering healthy intellectual and emotional patterns than are strategies of direct cognitive stimulation" (Greenspan, 1997, p. 14).

One morning, as Wesley enjoyed getting horseback rides from Denise, his classmates were watching with great anticipation. His peers began to ask for a turn as well. Denise took the small group to a movement room, and each child waited for a turn. When told that it was another student's turn and that he would have to wait, Wesley threw himself on the floor and wailed. When asked, "What do you want?" Wesley eventually made the sign for more. The other children decided that they did not want to wait either, and that they could give rides to one another. Wesley and his friends enjoyed riding on Denise's back, riding one another's backs, and giving each other horseback rides. Wesley made and sustained eye contact, smiled, and giggled. As the group laughed with and signed more to one another, they decided to make tickets so that more children could play Wesley's horse-riding game.

Wesley's passion for and competence in gross motor games led to connections with the friends that shared those same interests. Following their collective interests promoted Wesley's increasing comfort level with peers. The children within the group who created tickets used problem-solving, social negotiation, and fine motor skills to overcome the issue of waiting for turns. The work of each of those children moved forward that day.

Wesley continued to make further social connections with the other children that year, and he began to make some one–to–one connections as well. One day as Wesley was enjoying time in a closed, quiet space, another child was playing with a round, wooden bead. The child dropped the bead and it rolled under Wesley's table. To the child's surprise, the bead came rolling right back out! After rolling the ball under the table and watching it come back a couple of times, he looked to see what was under the table! It was his friend, Wesley! (See Figure 1.1.)

Wesley was delighted to play this mash-up game of hide-and-seek, peek-a-boo, and catch! The teachers also discovered that Wesley continued to demonstrate strong interests in the natural world. He loved looking at sunlight and the wind in the trees and would gather petals and leaves. Wesley enjoyed the feel, sound, or smell of autumn leaves, so Sara created a sensory bin of leaves in her room. Wesley enjoyed interacting with the bin so much that he climbed right in! Wesley was joined by another child, who was also a naturalist. Together, they became involved in and enjoyed Wesley's in-depth exploration of the autumn leaves!

Denise observed that if teachers attempted to have Wesley move away from the sunlight in the window in order to complete a teacher-directed task, he would become very distressed and agitated. Denise took this challenge and decided to use Wesley's interest in the sunlight to move his work forward. While attending a study tour in Reggio Emilia, Italy, Denise heard a story about a child who was fascinated by light. The staff there decided to play games with her interest and record the child's reactions. They gave her a flashlight and let her draw with the beam in a dark room; they offered acetate, markers, and an overhead projector so that her drawing would be projected by light. They also offered teacher-drawn shapes on dark paper, and when the child pinpointed holes along the shape, the light shone through the edges. As you can envision, her work was moving from gross- to fine-motor representations.

One overriding message given to those attending the study tour was to look at frustration and hindrance as possibility. Denise accepted that invitation as she thought about moving Wesley's communication, interactions, and skill development forward. She attached translucent acetate to the window and made paints and brushes available. Wesley held a paintbrush and painted

Figure 1.1. Wesley and Child

Figure 1.2. Wesley Painting at Window

on the acetate with the sun shining in through his work. Teachers would then offer painting to Wesley when he chose to sit in the sunlight of the window-sill. Eventually Wesley began to request painting with his PECS card. An easel was placed near the window. Wesley both finger-painted and brush-painted on the paper attached to the easel. He was close to the sunlight that he found so attractive, yet was able to move his painting work forward onto an easel (see Figure 1.2).

Not only had Wesley's communicative and cognitive development moved forward, the other children began to show interest as well. They were clearly attracted to the concept of painting on clear paper attached to a window. They became most engaged, however, when they began to recognize the subject of Wesley's paintings. "It looks like a KABOOM!" a child announced about one of Wesley's paintings. "Who painted the grasshopper?" another asked. When we looked closely at another of Wesley's paintings we could clearly see lines that formed the shape of a grasshopper's body and legs! Children began to ask to paint near and with Wesley. Diagnosed with autism and with limited verbal capabilities, Wesley had made many friendships with other children interested in sharing their common love of nature.

EMBRACING RISKS: ADOPTING THE PROJECT APPROACH

Imagine a teacher who gives her- or himself permission to teach through an emergent curriculum, learning through attempts and failures, as well as successes. Imagine if this teacher discovered the interests and intelligences of each child and determined that these are parts of each child's unique strengths. Imagine if this teacher taught with those strengths and engaged each child in her or his care. Imagine if the teacher created an environment in the classroom in which every child could confidently learn with his or her own strengths as well as respect and learn from the strengths of the other children. Finally, imagine the possibilities if children, parents, and teachers learned with and from one another.

Marty Gravett was a new lead teacher at The Sabot School. She was hired for many reasons, one of which was her obvious enthusiasm for a method of teaching young children that was new to the United States. She had been to Reggio Emilia, Italy, and was taken by this method of thinking about teaching young children. In the Reggio Emilia schools, the educators gather research on early learning and create environments that are developmentally best for young children, families, educators, and communities. In these schools, evidence-based best practices form the didactic learning environment. Postwar Reggio Emilia, Italy, was committed to creating learning environments that were based upon the essential respect for children's active, inquisitive, and vitally creative engagement with the world.

Loris Malaguzzi, who was the founder of the Reggio Emilia schools, coined the term *the hundred languages of children* in order to speak to the philosophy that each child has multiple avenues by which to learn and grow and to express their knowledge, creativity, and social competence. In the Reggio schools, learning is designed to be evolving and is negotiated with the children according to the mutual interests of teachers and students. This differs from the typical curriculum in America, where units of study are generally predetermined according to the time of year and are planned primarily by the teacher. The Reggio schools encourage collaborative planning that involves all staff members, the students themselves, and, at times, the families of the student.

Malaguzzi (Edwards, Gandini, & Forman, 1993) wrote:

> The wider the range of possibilities we offer children, the more intense will be their motivations and the richer their experiences. We must widen the range of topics and goals, the types of situations we offer and their degree of structure, the kinds and combinations of resources and materials, and the possible interactions with things, peers, and adults. (p. 73)

Malaguzzi sought to conceptualize educators as the children, families, staff, and community who create environments that promote and facilitate learning for all. The foundation of the Reggio Emilia approach is a profound respect for the child's active, inquisitive, and vitally creative engagement with the world.

Malaguzzi speaks of children's "surprising and extraordinary strengths and capabilities" being "linked with an inexhaustible need for expression and realization" (Edwards et al., p. 72). Here we are encouraged to shift our thinking further. Not only are teachers permitted to relinquish their traditional role of filling the children with predetermined knowledge that is age-appropriate, but all participants may respect and celebrate children as experienced and competent researchers in life. For some children, this competence will be found beyond their abilities to learn to read and calculate at school. In contrast to Americans' emphasis on logical and verbal skills, the schools in Reggio Emilia cultivate the hundred languages of children: the numerous artistic and kinesthetic (as well as verbal) ways in which children make meaning of their experience and express their differences.

When Marty came to The Sabot School, she soon found herself at a staff meeting attempting to help the staff to see and perhaps share her vision of bringing the Reggio philosophy home to Sabot and incorporating Reggio practices in how we worked with our young children. However, hiring someone to be a visionary and making that vision a reality were two different things. Marty was essentially asking the staff to take risks in their teaching. This was scary stuff and raised a lot of questions for the staff, such as: What did she mean, begin the year without any extensive plans or curriculum and instead observe children to determine their interests? How would staff know what to do? Where would ideas for activities and lessons come from? How would teachers provide the children with the skills they needed for kindergarten readiness? How would they know what students had learned and what they needed to learn if no units or themes were planned and if they did not concentrate on the skills and lessons they had been taught were important in early childhood education? But eventually the true fear of the staff members was revealed: What if they failed at this new method of teaching?

At that point, Marty won over many of the staff and eliminated their doubts. She explained that there would be no fear of failure in this method, that what might normally be considered a failure, such as an activity that bombs, an idea that falls flat, and so forth, is just one more step in the process of discovery. Marty explained that the staff would become co-constructors of knowledge with the children in their classes, and this would give the staff permission to rethink the role of teachers. This role change was from the teacher as the imparter of knowledge to the teacher as one who provides children with the necessary support to make discoveries and learn in a more cooperative manner. Staff members would become facilitators of learning for the children, the families, one another, and themselves as individuals. The staff began to see that this philosophy of cooperative learning and rethinking failure made sense. After all, is it a failed lesson if a child tries to build with blocks in a new way and they fall down, or if the child falls the first time he or she walks on a balance beam? Of course not; that's how they learn. Couldn't the staff make the same allowances for their own learning process? In addition, as co-constructors of knowledge with the children, teachers are also given permission to revisit and learn from failures. This simple idea created such a sense of freedom for the staff at The Sabot School. The chance to try new ways of engaging and teaching children with no fear of failure, but rather an attitude of learning as a process, was an exciting and freeing notion.

An additional and important part of this notion came from the under-standing that as a staff, there was no competition for success or shame in failure. Everyone was in this together and there for one another. After engaging in multiple experiences of working together and teaching in this manner, the staff began to understand that the process of observing children and exploring with them and other teachers to determine children's interests and strengths taught them more about these children, and what they know, or need to know, than they had ever been aware of before.

Teachers discovered that going beyond the unit approach allowed them to teach children social negotiation and self-construction skills more easily. They began to understand that using the unit approach alone, with the specific planning of activities designed by the unit, or according to the teacher's ideas and agenda, did not emerge from the strengths or interests of the children or sufficiently reflect the children's differing levels of competency. Through this process the daily experiences of the staff affirmed that children truly do learn through many avenues, interests, and intelligence—or languages, as the teachers in the Reggio Emilia schools would say.

FOLLOWING CHILDREN'S INTERESTS: MALLORY'S STORY

One such child at Sabot was Mallory, who needed teachers to look beyond the typical methods of introducing and reinforcing concepts and skills in the early childhood environment. Mallory had a great imagination, which led the staff to identify her as a master player, with the ability to organize, plan, and carry out elaborate story lines and engage other children in her play. This was great, and the staff recognized her strength in symbolic play. However, Mallory was not interested in stopping that play and attending to teacher-initiated or teacher-led learning activities centered around some of the kindergarten readiness skills and proficiencies that she needed to develop. Persistent attempts by teachers to get her to settle into some of these activities resulted in Mallory complaining, resisting, sighing mightily, or trying to get a classmate distracted from what they were doing—in essence, she was doing everything but learning.

Debbie was fortunate to be teaching at Sabot, where there was an environment conducive to true team input, support, and collaboration. At the weekly staff meetings teachers were given the opportunity to discuss, dissect, and problem-solve with one another about every facet of teaching young children. (As one of our teachers, Anna Golden, declared, "Together we're a genius!") At our next staff meeting Debbie brought up the dilemma she was feeling about Mallory. Debbie wanted to validate Mallory's strengths in the dramatic play realm, but needed her to also have an opportunity to practice those skills that she tended to avoid, in particular fine motor and pre-literacy tasks. It was also difficult to get Mallory to follow through and stay with activities for an extensive amount of time. Our team leader, Marty, asked a pivotal question:

Why was Mallory avoiding those tasks? Was it a lack of interest or low skill level that created her need to avoid them? As Debbie considered this question she realized that Mallory really was not very skilled in these areas, which was a contradiction to her primary persona; one of a strong, outgoing, intelligent, and competent little girl. Perhaps it was difficult for her to work on something in which she felt unsuccessful. What might motivate her enough to want to tackle such tasks?

In thinking about Mallory's penchant for the dramatic, coupled with the fact that Debbie thoroughly enjoyed this venue of self-expression herself, she began to see the possibility of using one of Mallory's strongest languages, dramatic play, to support her in going further in the skill areas in which she was challenged. Debbie asked Mallory if she would like to create a story for a movie that could be videotaped. Mallory thought that was a fabulous idea and was very excited at the prospect! Debbie created certain conditions that Mallory had to adhere to for this project to go further. If Mallory was to create a movie, she had to be the director, producer, and prop person, and she had to take on the tasks and responsibilities that went along with those roles. Mallory willingly took on that challenge. In the process of creating a video about a princess and the bad guy knights over a 3-week period of time, Mallory was required to:

1. Dictate a story that had a beginning, a middle, and an end
2. Cast her movie, which entailed
   » Making a list of characters
   » Writing (with teacher help) a list of those characters
   » Recruiting actors and negotiating who would take on which roles
   » Writing actors' names (with teacher help) to correspond with characters
3. Decide, along with the other actors, what kind of props were needed (another opportunity to practice negotiation skills)
4. Make the props, which involved planning, and extensive fine-motor skills such as cutting, gluing, drawing, writing, sewing, etc.
5. Create communications that notified actors of practice times
6. Make signs advertising show times
7. Create tickets to the show
8. Sell tickets to the show

Mallory created a fabulous movie that was the hit of the year at Sabot School! More important, however, was the confidence she gained in following through on challenging tasks in order to achieve her goal of making a movie. As a result of using Mallory's strengths and interests as a springboard for learning, the staff noticed a significant difference in Mallory's willingness to attempt new skills as well as an improvement in her actual abilities. An unexpected bonus was the increase in skill level of the children who were participants in the moviemaking project.

AN INTEREST-BASED PROJECT: IS MISS STEPHANIE A PIRATE?

The following project illustrates a process that originated from the case of 3-year-old Brent, who received speech services in an inclusive preschool class. At the beginning of the year Miss Stephanie, the speech therapist, told the children that she had a treasure chest the students could choose a gift from after they had completed a certain number of speech tasks. Brent came back to his regular class very excited and wondered aloud whether Miss Stephanie might be a pirate! The teacher, Debbie, had had several years experience in working in the project approach by now, and realized immediately that the level of excitement and speculation that rippled throughout the class was worth exploring. Soon afterward she realized that the class had just found the first project of the year, and she was comfortable with putting the apple unit she had preplanned in reserve for another time! The following story provides some examples of how Debbie used this very exciting child-initiated unit to teach skills in the classroom. To begin the investigation, the class read books about pirates in order to determine what clues to look for in determining whether Miss Stephanie was, indeed, a pirate.

Skills and Concepts Embedded Within the Project

This aspect of the investigation process allowed the class to work on a number of skills: listening, seeing ideas in print, comprehension, memory, wh- questions (what, where, when, etc.), and the very scientific concept of prediction. The children came up with a list of pirate traits:

1. Treasure chest
2. A parrot
3. An eye patch
4. A sword
5. A pirate flag
6. A pirate map

In the spirit of pirating, the children began their research by going to the library and getting out books about maps in order to find the way to Miss Stephanie's office and look for those clues. Children participated at their own specific levels of development, some making intricate maps, some following the lines of the map with their fingers, and others pointing out pictures or actions in the book while some children were tracking with their eyes to indicate which way the arrow was pointing. Debbie provided the class with opportunities to notice how maps look from different perspectives by photographing a town the children built from blocks: first from the front of the town and again from above.

In one of the books the students read, a child had made a map of her room. The children in the class found this to be a great idea and began to

Figure 1.3. Making a Map to Miss Stephanie's Room

make maps of their own, including a map of one section of their room, the housekeeping area. Afterward children drew a map to Miss Stephanie's room. (See Figure 1.3)

The children were challenged by Debbie to come up with questions to ask Miss Stephanie that would let them know when she would not be in her office. Once that information was gathered, the class took the map and sneaked down the hall to her room. The map confirmed that they had indeed reached Miss Stephanie's office! Once inside Miss Stephanie's office, the children were reminded to keep their eyes open for clues, using their list of pirate traits as a guide. The children found a pirate map, a telescope, and a pirate hat, and one child even noticed there was a ship on Miss Stephanie's wall calendar! And the biggest clue of all: a treasure chest! Based on those clues, the children came up with questions to ask Miss Stephanie to determine whether she was, in fact, a pirate. (See Figure 1.4.) These questions were straightforward, as you might expect from a group of preschoolers:

Are you a real pirate?
Can we play with your pirate stuff?
Can we have one treasure from your treasure chest?

As a result of their questions, the children found out that Miss Stephanie was not actually a real pirate; she was only gathering items for a pirate costume for Halloween! Graciously, she did allow the children to pick one treasure from the treasure box!

The excitement of the research, conjecture, and problem-solving about the connection between Miss Stephanie and pirates spilled over into other centers of the room, such as the building area, art area, and dramatic play area. Children used various problem-solving strategies and social negotiations

Figure 1.4. Kids
with Ms.
Stephanie

Figure 1.5.
Destiny with
Ship

to create pirate ships with planks, which took a lot of problem-solving; and introduced the idea of ramps, balance, and very importantly, some meaningful cooperative play. Intricate castles were created with children sharing their strengths with others and some children gained the realization of using blocks to represent, rather than just build and knock down, which had been a problem prior to this activity. Children also were provided open-ended materials in the art area, and they began to create pirate ships, which proved to be a great opportunity for peer-modeling and scaffolding strategies.

At the end of the project, the documentation taken of the children's work was gathered. The documentation consisted of products that had been created by the children, such as pirate ships, maps, lists, signs, and so forth (see Figure 1.5). However, it also consisted of documentation that provided evidence of the processes involved in the project, such as pictures of block-building, children negotiating in dramatic play, problem-solving between peers, and children involved in sharing books and ideas. Conversations and questions between children and with children and teachers that were recorded or written at the time were also a part of the documentation.

Meeting Curriculum Objectives

These pieces of documentation provided the materials for an amazing bulletin board display that reflected the work of the children during that time. It also provided the teachers with the information to consider the skills, concepts, and development had taken place during those few weeks. During that project period the class engaged in multiple curriculum objectives. For those who wonder if dedicating several weeks to a pirate project was worth the time and energy, the following list, organized by objective, might provide some answers:

Science. Science was addressed through the children's: collecting information through research, predicting outcomes, proposing hypotheses, gathering evidence, and comparing information. The children learned the concept of balance and created ramps in building, investigated the concept of comparing objects of same/different sizes, and used their various senses to explore an environment.

Pre-literacy. Pre-literacy skills were addressed through students' dictating and creating lists with teachers and one another. Making maps not only provided the children with the opportunity to create lines and practice perceptual motor skills, it also provided them an understanding of how symbols can represent something meaningful. In addition, children who were developmentally ready were able to print letters and assign names to the drawings on their maps. Children used books to find and compare information, describe actions, and retell and act out pirate stories, which provided practice in sequencing, memory, and reading comprehension.

Early Math. Early math skills were represented in drawing lines in perspective, measuring, making charts for comparing what pirates use versus what the children's parents use in daily life, using geometric shapes, collecting data, and counting in a meaningful manner (i.e., how many steps are there from the classroom to Miss Stephanie's office?).

Personal-Social Skills. The personal-social skills that were being developed as this project proceeded are perhaps the most important skills the children acquired. Children were provided with support by the teachers to plan, discuss, negotiate, and follow through with tasks. Children were provided with the language needed to help them in their ability to negotiate with peers. Children were encouraged to use each other as resources, and they were provided the opportunity to notice an area of strength in a peer that would enable a more likely chance to create bonds. This ability was especially important when the peer that exhibited such strengths was challenged in other areas, which might have prevented his or her peer from recognizing their commonalities. As a result of this project, children's level of play was challenged, and many children in the class naturally moved from one level of play to the next developmental level.

Fine-Motor Skills. Fine-motor skills were employed as the children cut, glued, built, drew, balanced, and created structures.

SUMMARY

As early childhood special educators, we have come to understand that the potential for children of all abilities to learn and develop successfully is dependent on our understanding and respect for these children's differences and strengths and how they affect the learning process. It is not enough to follow through on pre-developed plans of teaching without a consideration of the whole child, including the child's behaviors and sense of self. We have to ask ourselves on a regular basis, what is the child trying to communicate to me? Is this behavior something that should be extinguished, or is there a message waiting to be discovered by all those who are working with the child?

Supporting children in their ability to connect with others and in their attempts to self-regulate can sometimes take a back seat to learning the lessons. Yet, it is our belief that these connections are the basis for all learning, and, if given the time, that nurturing such connections will accelerate learning. The strengths-based project approach allows educators to discover the many strengths of children with special needs and allows those children to blossom in their thinking, planning, and creativity through project work.

As evidenced in this chapter, it is very possible to address children's skills, concepts, and objectives while at the same time allowing the children's interests to guide and inform the teacher's planning. The real accomplishment in the pirate project is that all the children were invested and interested in the exploration and learning. While the teachers certainly created plans regarding the day's activities, they were open to new ideas and flexible enough to change plans when it was appropriate. The investment of the children in the class proved to be an incentive to complete tasks that they might have balked at normally. It is interesting to think about what difference there might have been in those few weeks of learning if the teacher, rather than listening to the children's rich conversations, wondering, and excitement about the prospect of Miss Stephanie being a pirate, had instead said something such as: "Of course she's not a pirate, Brent. Settle down, and let's sing a song." Would Brent have been devastated? Probably not. Would he have been discouraged? Perhaps so. Certainly the originally planned apple project would not have produced the same excitement and investment in the experiences that the impromptu pirate unit did.

CHAPTER 2

Identifying Each Child's Strengths

There is much we need to learn about each child in order to implement a strengths-based approach to teaching. Even before the first day of school, staff members may begin the process of learning about the children's strengths, including their interests, skills, and intelligences. This chapter will offer strategies, tools, and checklists for gathering and organizing valuable information about each child from the family, the child's special education team, and the school's confidential files. It offers advice on how to prepare data collection forms so all adults involved can continue to get to know each child from the very first days of school through the end of the year.

SCHEDULING TIME TO LEARN ABOUT EACH CHILD

While planning for and scheduling the time before the school year begins, policy makers, district and board members, administrators, service providers, and families have the opportunity to prioritize discovering each child's strengths. Typically, educators and therapists spend much of the week before the school year begins attending meetings and in-service trainings. It is expected that teachers and therapists will spend what little time remains of the week decorating the environment, sorting through materials and supplies, and completing lesson plans for the week. While these practices ready the traditional aesthetics of the environment and prepare for the traditional theme-based instruction, they leave little to no time or energy to focus on the process of preparing to know and work with each child.

As early childhood educators, we are keenly aware of the need for educational communities to budget the time and the resources for getting to know each child's present strengths and needs before the children arrive. To follow recommended best practices, staff need time to contact families, make home visits, and read each child's updated confidential school folder in order to organize and utilize all of the information before the children arrive (Sandall et al., 2005). Armed with this understanding of their incoming students, teachers are better able to prepare the environment to engage each child's strengths and meet each child's needs. This type of preparedness before the children arrive provides a strong foundation for learning throughout the school year.

LEARNING FROM FAMILIES

The Division of Early Childhood (DEC) of the Council for Exceptional Children reinforces the need to work with families in gaining and then using information about children in their guide of recommended practices:

> Effective family-based practices move beyond simply identifying the strengths and assets of children and families to using these strengths and assets as building blocks for acquiring new information and skills. (Sandall et al., 2005, p. 111)

> Begin discovering each child's strengths from those who know their child best, the family. First, families provide valuable authentic and longitudinal information about their child not otherwise available. . . . . Further; family members provide needed information about their circumstances and the possible impact on the child. (Sandall et al., 2005, p. 46)

Through living with and caring for their child, families know their child to an extent that neither any experienced teacher nor any comprehensive evaluation could ever match. They have lived through their child's health concerns, life experiences, interventions, development, and relationships. Families know how well their child is able to function at home and in the community. All families have seen their child's skills, interests, preferences, comfort levels, communication styles, challenges, fears, discomforts, dislikes, and learning styles.

The DEC hails family-centered practices for serving young children with challenges. The DEC Recommended Practices emphasizes the critical role of families in their definition of family-based practices which is

> a philosophy or way of thinking that leads to a set of practices in which families or parents are considered central and the most important decision maker in a child's life. More specifically it recognizes that the family is the constant in a child's life and that service systems and personnel must support, respect, encourage, and enhance the strengths and competence of the family. (Sandall et al., 2005. p. 119)

As educators, we acknowledge that intense and sustained in-the-role training qualifies families to answer the screening and assessment questions that will identify the sensory integration, emotional, social, communication, adaptive, cognitive, and motor functioning of their child. Yet, too often, listening to families ends there.

Families conduct countless informal assessments as they attempt to meet their child's needs and to help their child function in the family. They experiment with various routines, accommodations, and supports. They spend years cutting the tags out of shirts so that the scratchy edges do not aggravate their child. They diligently cook special meals because their child is a picky eater.

They referee every peer or sibling interaction. They translate their child's attempts to communicate to other people. They tirelessly repeat the same directions or make reminder cards with pictures to help their child learn new routines. The literature confirms that parental reports are a valid measure of children's capabilities (Harte, 2009). The results of each family's informal assessments and modifications provide a wealth of pertinent information about strategies used to support their child's self-regulation and developmental needs and strengths. This cache of information is ready and available to be put to use before the school year even begins!

In fact, families are the only ones who have this depth of experience with their child. The moment a child becomes a member of a family, the family begins to know him or her. As each child develops and ventures out to meet extended family, doctors, friends, early interventionists, neighbors, babysitters, therapists, day-care providers, or playmates, everyone looks to the family to communicate for their child. Families need to continue providing this valuable service for their child as he or she enters school and meets the educators and therapists who will work with him or her for anywhere from 6 hours per day to 30 minutes per week (Mitchell & Hauser-Cram, 2009; Xu, 2008).

STRATEGIES FOR LEARNING FROM FAMILIES

Schools often host open houses so that each child and family has a chance to meet the teachers, classmates, and school administration they will be working with in the coming school year, as well as to allow the child to see his or her classroom before the year begins. Some environments offer parent orientations to provide policy and procedural information and to address questions. These gatherings give families the opportunity to hear from the service providers and gather information. Yet, typically, administrators design and format these meetings in such a manner that they miss a valuable opportunity to listen to and learn from the families about their child.

Personal Information Questionnaire. Some environments send questionnaires to families asking about their child's strengths and challenges. These questionnaires typically use a write-in, short-answer format. They might ask about each child's specific preferences. Sample questions might include:

- Describe your child's typical behavior when he or she separates from you.
- Does your child typically carry a transition object when separating from you or your home? What is that object?
- What does your child typically choose to enjoy during quiet time?
- What are your child's favorite books, songs, and activities?

These questionnaires often focus on the information that families have that will help their child transition from home to school. This information is especially pertinent during the early childhood years when each child is acclimating to the separations from family and from the routines of home.

We propose that schools consider broadening the scope of questionnaires for families. Questions that will encourage families to share all that they have learned and discovered about their child over the years might include:

- How would you describe your child's temperament? (Providing a short list of different temperaments may help families to recognize those characteristics.)
- What strategies have you found helpful when teaching your child a new or challenging skill?
- How does your child soothe and regulate him- or herself when upset?
- What specific materials or activities does your child usually avoid?

Such specific information will support each child to feel understood and competent and will inform her or his strengths-based program.

However, it is also important to keep the questionnaire manageable. The questions need to be prioritized, concise, and open-ended. Again, the short-answer format allows each family the freedom to share what they know about their child. This format also allows the family to decide what information is most important to share. Families will be less restricted in what they deem significant information and as a result, open communication will begin to flow. (See Appendix A for a sample parent questionnaire)

Multiple Intelligences Form. Howard Gardner offers that there are eight intelligences: Linguistic, Logical-Mathematical, Spatial, Bodily-Kinesthetic, Musical, Intrapersonal, Interpersonal, and Natural. He defines Multiple Intelligence Theory as "the plurality of intelligences" (Gardner, 1993).

Gardner goes on to speak to the fact that individuals differ in the particular intelligence profiles with which they are born and that the purpose of school should be to develop intelligences and to help people reach vocational and avocational goals that are appropriate to their particular intelligences. If our schools could recognize children's differing intelligences and tailor instruction to meet those intelligences, children would in turn feel more engaged and competent, and therefore more inclined to serve the society in a constructive way (Gardner, 1993).

The Multiple Intelligences form (Appendix B) specifically offers information about Howard Gardner's theoretical work on acknowledging and fostering the multiple ways that each child may manifest or channel his or her intelligences. The form also seeks to enhance each family's awareness of their child's intellectual and processing strengths in light of these multiple intelligences, and to share their perspectives with the teachers and therapists.

The Multiple Intelligences form organizes and identifies activities typical-ly preferred by children as they express their intelligences. This form also pro-vides families, teachers, and therapists with descriptions of how a child might best use each intelligence in the learning process. For example, a child who possesses a musical intelligence may prefer to engage in singing, humming, or playing instruments, and may learn best by putting the new information or task to music or rhythmic movements. The Multiple Intelligences form invites families to reflect upon what they have observed and discerned about their child. Families might ask themselves what they have noticed about their child's preferences and interests. They might think back to times when they have taught their child or have observed their child learning. They might try to recall what strategies they or their child used to acquire and retain new in-formation. They may think about their child's current interests, preferences, and chosen modes of learning.

Families often report that this form served to enhance their awareness of their child's intellectual and processing strengths in light of these multiple intelligences. In turn, families are able to then share their perspectives with the teachers and therapists.

Gatherings to Complete Forms and Exchange Information. Some schools are now offering gatherings to families. The prospective student visits the well-staffed class and enjoys playing and a snack, while the adult family members hear from the administration, ask questions, and fill out surveys and question-naires about their child's strengths and needs. One choice might be to hold an evening meeting as part of your family–school connection. Evening meetings typically allow families to come after work hours and to concentrate on gain-ing and providing information for the benefit of their child (see Appendix C).

LEARNING FROM THE COLLABORATIVE TEAM

Turnbull, Turnbull, Erwin, and Soodak (2006) describe the eight functions of a family. Families are responsible for providing: affection, self-esteem, spiritual-ity, economics, daily care, socialization, recreation, and education. Time and energy are required to meet and provide these functions.

Most of us can relate to the demands of meeting these needs for ourselves or for our families. Therefore, we can appreciate the stress created when com-pounding these demands with those of caring for a child with developmental needs and challenges (Koplow, 2007; Mitchell & Hauser-Cram, 2009; Osborne & Reed, 2009; Parish, Rose, & Andrews, 2010; Parish, Rose, Grinstein-Weiss, Richman, & Andrews, 2008).

It also is important to remember that for families with young children, and especially for families with children who have challenges, carving time and en-ergy to fill out and return forms can feel overwhelming. The thought of finding child care, or packing up the children and bringing them to the school to fill out forms, or to visit the classroom, may seem insurmountable. In addition to these typical concerns faced by families with young children, working families may have to arrange for time off from their jobs and possibly ask child care providers to take their children early or to keep them late. With so many responsibilities and such demands on their time and energy, families may feel hesitant or unavailable to interact or even communicate with therapists and educators.

Therefore, the key to strong communication is not just the type of form used or the format used to meet and share information. Rather, the emphasis is on developing respectful and reciprocal communication amongst all who work with the child (Cheatham & Ostrosky, 2009). Although all forms may not specifically ask a question that is pertinent to each child and his or her family, family members who feel that their judgment is valued by their child's team will feel more inclined to call, e-mail, or send a note to the other members with their thoughts. For example, a questionnaire may not ask about any traumatic experiences the child has endured. Yet, we all know the effect that such an experience has on young children. So, although the form used did not specifically ask about traumatic experiences, a family member who considers him- or herself to be an integral member of the team knows how pertinent this information is to the child's functioning at home and may realize that her team members at school will need this information as well. Just as families share new developments with Grandma and other members of their extended family, families in partnership with educators and therapists will realize that they need to share new developments or pertinent experiences with their school family as well.

Strategies for Learning from the Team

The intent is to follow an interdisciplinary model, which is defined in the DEC Recommended Practices as: "Professionals from multiple professional disciplines who represent special expertise working together to help children with disabilities and their families accomplish important outcomes" (Sandall et al., 2005, pp. 127–128).

Creating a Transdisciplinary Team. While the intent of early childhood special education is to work in interdisciplinary teams, children, families, educators, and therapists benefit most when they form transdisciplinary teams. In their book, *Empowered Families, Successful Children* (2000), Susan Epps and Barbara Jackson define a transdisciplinary team as one in which

the family, educators, therapists, social workers, medical personnel, psychologists, and/or administrators, collaborate as a team to assess, plan, and implement what is best for the child. The members of the team, which interacts in a transdisciplinary manner, release their roles and expertise and strive to inform and train all, so that each member of the team may feel confident and competent in continually supporting each child's well-being and development, whether at home, in the clinical setting, at school, or out in the community. (pp. 107–108)

In this sense, not only do the parents need to share their expertise about their child with the other team members, they also benefit when available and ready to learn from the expertise of the therapists, educators, and administrators on the team (Jung, 2007).

Communication takes time and effort on the part of the families, educators, and therapists. A key to opening communication is to build trust and rapport within the relationship with each family. A family may speak a different language, practice cultural norms, or have political and religious beliefs that diverge from your own. Yet, when the intent of the interactions is to provide child-focused and caregiver-focused interventions, the team promotes a climate of respect, which shifts the focus from any philosophical or cultural differences to providing for the child and the family based upon their preferences (Branson & Bingham, 2009; Xu, 2008). This author remembers a quote which a minister shared with his congregation. The minister would remind the congregation that "People don't care what you know until they know that you care."

Creating Trust Practices. Ann and Rud Turnbull, Elizabeth Erwin, and Leslie Soodak (2006) emphasize the need to build trust amongst the members when forming a team. They define trust as

> having confidence in someone else's reliability, judgment, word, and action to care for and not harm the entrusted person. It exists when people believe that the trusted person will act in the best interest of the person extending the trust and will make good faith efforts to keep their word. (p. 161)

Turnbull and colleagues further delineate four Trust Practices: Be reliable, use sound judgment, maintain confidentiality, and trust yourself (pp. 162–163). They offer that maintaining these four trust practices enables us to create and gain trust in our partnerships with team members.

Being Reliable. Being reliable means fulfilling your responsibilities, which necessitates taking on only those responsibilities that you are willing to devote the time, energy, and persistence needed to carry them through to fruition. Team members should document all plans to meet goals, including who is responsible and when the goal is expected to be completed (Scholtes, Joiner, & Streibel, 2003). A simple form may be created with three headings: goal, responsible person, and due date. This form enables the entire team to check in with the responsible person and offer assistance if needed. Goals that the team intends to meet might include tasks such as: referring a child for assistive technology services, researching assistive technology devices, and contacting community resources and supports for the family. It is, of course, important to acknowledge and respect the time and energy constraints that each team member faces. The team may openly discuss and plan for opportunities to ask for an extension on due dates, to delegate responsibilities, or to bring tasks back to the group for reevaluation if the responsible team member has not been able to fulfill her or his duty.

Using Sound Judgment. Using sound judgment involves remaining amenable to debate and then jointly making decisions as an informed team. It is our responsibility to each child to not only stay informed of the latest research pertaining to child development and pedagogical and other practices, but also to critically evaluate the relevancy as well as the applicability of the research to our strengths-based program. This, in turn, will enhance or support the work of the team. Another factor in using sound judgment is communication. If the team discusses and pre-plans options for a child, all team members need to be involved in the decision-making process.

Adrienne Martin, a mother who has teamed with both of the authors in using the strengths-based approach, reflects on her son Shep's early childhood education experiences now that he is attending elementary school:

> For several years after noticing Shep's sensory and auditory processing issues, we tried on some level to get to the bottom of it all. We sought out specialists who could diagnose him so that we could better help him—and so that we might know what the future would hold. While medical and professional feedback has been very important to us, we have slowly realized that Shep does not fit a diagnosis per se. He is his own very strong and joyful being—so much more than a simple diagnosis can convey. As we have gained more and more experience with children with exceptional needs, we have realized that each and every child is truly unique—and that diagnoses can be very limiting. They can lead people to make assumptions about the child and the assumptions are often inaccurate. Shep is just Shep—and he is perfect to us.
>
> Some of the ways we have tried to emphasize Shep's many positive qualities with therapists and educators include:
>
> - When meeting a new therapist or teacher, we like to lead with his strengths. First of all, because that's what we truly feel, but also, it's a way to set that precedent with the therapist and educator—and to let them know that we expect the same from them—thinking about his strengths first and his challenges second.
> - When communicating with therapists and educators, we like to speak about Shep's interests and social interactions throughout the session so that all of the emphasis of the therapy or education is not exclusively on academic/therapeutic goals.
> - During a therapy session, we are very conscious about speaking in positive terms about what has transpired since our last visit. If we tell a story to the therapist, we try to encourage Shep to give

his input as well. If I have a concern to express, we try to do it over the phone or via e-mail.

- We also try to involve Shep's younger brother in his therapy sessions as often as possible. We feel that this normalizes the experience for both boys.

- When Shep attended a private preschool, we asked our occupational therapist and speech therapist to see him once a week in the school setting. Other children were encouraged to be a part of the sessions. Once again, bringing therapy into the school normalized the treatment for Shep and made it possible for our life after school to be filled with more enriching, nontherapy experiences.

- When attending IEP (Individualized Education Program) meetings, where the level of the child's performance and the goals for the upcoming year are presented), we find it extremely beneficial to begin the meeting with a description of our experience of Shep at home. We think this helps to give the IEP team a deeper understanding of him and helps them remember what is wonderful about him rather than merely focusing on his academic struggles.

Recently Shep was encountering some teasing at school about the way he talks. Two boys were imitating his speech in art class. We talked to Shep about it as he and his brother Lee were going to sleep one night. Lee simply said, "Mommy, they don't know it's okay to be different." We could not have been happier.

At Sabot, it felt as though everyone—from Irene, to his amazing teachers, to the parents, to the children—saw Shep as a whole child rather than a child with exceptional needs.

At Sabot, I felt as though we were all working together to help Shep thrive. The school was so incredibly flexible and accommodating. Teachers were always providing us with valuable insights, theories, and recommendations—almost daily. I have to say, the Sabot staff seemed much more informed and sophisticated in their understanding of Shep—much more so than either of the schools Shep has attended since. The teacher's constant quest for more knowledge and education about children was such a gift.

Maintaining Confidentiality. The fifth factor in developing trust with team-mates is maintaining confidentiality. The shift in a strengths-based program is from focusing on and planning to remediate each child's disabilities and weaknesses, to acknowledging and employing each child's capabilities and strengths. Yet, the depth of information that educators and therapists need to be aware of to best serve each child does require maintaining professionalism and confidentiality. Most administrations, educators, and therapists strive to uphold the ethics and standards of this field. We will all do well to remember to hold these same high standards outside of meetings with parents.

Educators and therapists benefit from hearing about what the families know about their children. Teaching is further enhanced by consulting with colleagues about teaching and therapeutic strategies. Discussing the needs of the children and their responsiveness to the implemented strategies supports all who work with children and families as professionals and as caring humans serving in early childhood special education.

Trusting Yourself. The final trust practice is Trust Yourself. It is both freeing and motivating as a team to develop the sense that there is no need to fear failure. With a transdisciplinary team's vast resources, expertise, and experiences, the team may trust that a wealth of evidence-based practices and strategies are available to implement through the process of serving each child. We add depth to our expertise when each member of the team strives to keep abreast of the latest research and regulations, tries strategies and observes the child's responsiveness, and realizes that we all are influenced by such factors as our gut feelings, cultural norms, faith, knowledge, experiences, constraints, and limits. We as educators need to approach our work with each child trusting that we have prepared for and will persistently strive to provide the best services.

Strategies for Communicating as a Team

As with every aspect of a program, it is critical to monitor the effectiveness of the communication among families, service providers, and administrators. Communication forms should be created with an awareness of each member of the team's level of literacy and dominant language. In addition, it is important as a team to be forthright with one another about which means of communication best meets everyone's time and energy needs as well as interests and intents. Families may differ on the extent of information they wish to communicate with the team and on what form of communication best meets their preferences. As a team, having or creating a variety of ways of communicating, as well as topics of communication, will lend to increased satisfaction for everyone.

Some effective modes of communication, collected over the years, include:

Home-to-School Journals. The use of journals offers another form of communication to members of the team. Families may start the journal at home with the child before he or she begins school. Families may include photos of themselves, family pets, their home, and the child's favorite items or of memorable events. Debbie suggests inviting the family to turn the notebook upside-down and backwards to begin writing from the back of the journal forward all of the details about their child that they know well and would like to share with the teachers and therapists.

Traveling Notebooks. A notebook can be used that travels back and forth daily with actual notes from families, educators, therapists, administrators, daycare providers, and so forth. Everyone involved with the child has access to and may respond to notes from everyone else on the team. Containing such correspondence in a composition notebook also provides a permanent record of what has transpired with each child. We suggest diligently dating and noting your name on each entry you make. Dating each entry creates a chronological record of information and data for use at conferences and IEP meetings, in progress reports, and so forth. By signing your name to every entry you have written, you identify yourself as a reference to all other members on the team. They will know to whom they should write a reply and whom they should thank for the fabulous insight and tips.

Preprinted Notes. Preprinted notes can be quickly filled in, yet have room to write more detailed notes as needed. These notes may go from school to home, providing the opportunity for all team members to read them before they travel home to the family. See a sample of a preprinted note in Figure 2.1 below.

Picture Cards. The technology that is available to create picture cards and symbols for children may also be used to send notes to the parents. Parents who

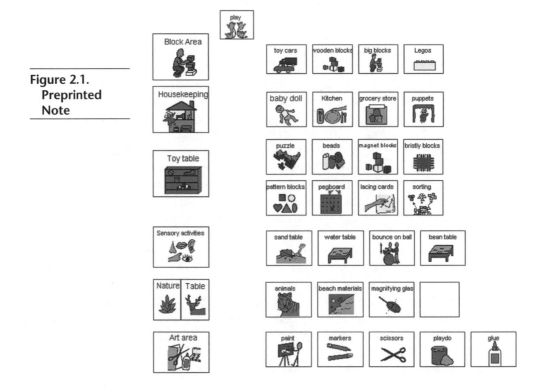

**Figure 2.1.
Preprinted
Note**

Figure 2.2. Picture Card. A picture card such as this can be used to communicate with parents. In this example, the note informs Danielle's parents that Danielle needs to bring more snack foods to school.

speak a language other than English or have limited literacy skills may become familiar with the picture symbols and use them to send general communication to the teachers. Samples of picture cards are illustrated in Figure 2.2.

Dry Erase Boards. Dry erase boards mounted in the halls offer a venue for the entire community to learn what is emerging in the classroom or special events or requests from the class.

CREATING SYSTEMS OF INFORMATION

Once you gather the valuable information about each child from the families, the confidential cumulative folders, and the other members of each child's team, it is time to organize all of the data so that they may be used to enhance the strengths-based education. Setting up the systems that organize information requires multiple considerations. It is important to think ahead and preplan.

Preplanning Communication Systems

At this point, having established the best ways to communicate with the families and the school, it is time to set up the home-to-school communication systems based upon the team members' needs. Teachers may use this time to request and acquire the home-to-school journals, generate daily pre-printed notes, or create picture cards and symbols that your students and their families might need for communication.

The use of your school's emergency contact information card provides access to a variety of ways of contacting each child's family and caregivers. You may also include a space on these cards for information such as the child's birthday and any known allergies so that you may to refer to them throughout the year. These cards can be discretely stored near the phone, door, or any other location where you might need them. If these data are not readily available through a computer from your home, a folder can be created with a copy of each contact/personal information card so that you can have access to all of its contents at home.

Preplanning Strengths and Interests Systems

Compiling the children's information on one form also helps to reveal which children share the same interests, whose strengths might support others', and who may serve as a consultant for small groups. Table 2.1 provides a sample of a Strengths, Learning Styles, and Intelligences Form. This chart organizes our knowledge that our student Liz has verbal/linguistic strengths and that she may be called upon to support those in the class who are interested in creating a picture book by telling the "story" of the book. If the children listening to the book decide to perform Liz's story, perhaps Laura, a visual-spatial student with a strong interest in art, will choose to make some props. In addition, Liz, Laura, and the adults have a pool of children who share their interests and whom they may invite to collaborate on the project. Having this information on one form will facilitate our work as we think about creating an environment in which each child begins to feel connected and as we scaffold relationships and form groups.

Creating Screening, Evaluation, and Assessment Results Systems

Assessment is used to determine the skills and information children have and under what conditions they are used. In addition, assessment procedures should determine the next level of skills and information that children should be acquiring; this information is critical in determining intervention targets. (Bricker, 2002. p. 11)

Table 2.1. Strengths, Intelligences, and Learning Styles

Child	Strengths	Intelligences	Learning Styles	Shared with:
Liz	Vocabulary, Stories	Verbal-Linguistic	Reading, Discussions	Kristen & Hannah
Kristen	Vocabulary, Stories	Verbal-Linguistic	Reading, Discussions	Liz & Hannah
Hannah	Vocabulary, Stories/ Drawings, Designs, Patterns, & Color	Verbal-Linguistic/ Visual-Spatial	Reading, Discussions, Art	Kristen & Liz/ Laura, Tess, Emma, & Charlie
Laura	Drawings, Designs, Patterns, & Color	Visual-Spatial	Art	Tess, Emma Hannah, & Charlie
Tess	Drawings, Designs, Patterns, & Color	Visual-Spatial	Art	Laura, Emma Hannah, & Charlie
Charlie	Drawings, Designs, Patterns, & Color	Visual-Spatial	Art	Tess, Emma Hannah, & Laura
Emma	Drawings, Designs, Patterns, & Color	Visual-Spatial	Art	Tess, Hannah, Charlie, & Laura

The information in a child's folder is confidential. Yet, knowing each child and respecting who each child is will create the optimal learning environment for everyone. The word respect is the key here. The learning environment established in the school is an essential element. An understanding of each child and adult and how they learn and work best alleviates the stigma and, at times, the restrictive connotations associated with confidential, disabilities, below-average skills, weaknesses, and so forth. While storage of confidential folders in the school vault assures parents that the contents of the folders will remain private, it also effectively guarantees that no one working with the child will have the time to refer to the valuable information it holds. It is important in the school community to devise a system that maintains the private nature of the information, yet insures that it is readily accessible to every one who works with the child. It does no good to gather the information for the children's folders if it is not further scrutinized, dissected, and put to use.

Any lists or charts that contain information from the confidential file should reflect appreciation for using each child's strengths to further her or his work. Not all data need to be charted and displayed on the classroom walls. When the parents, staff, and administration understand the value of making schedules, sensory diets, interests, and strengths more visible and accessible, they may feel more comfortable adopting practices that emphasize discretion when informing all members of the team. Information such as IEP objectives, behavior implementation program charts, and toileting or medicine schedules can be discretely filed yet visibly labeled and familiar to anyone who needs this information to support each child. For example, a teacher can create a sensory diet chart in a manner that emphasizes the role that such diets play in readying each child for their work and in grouping children with similar interests and needs.

Creating Systems for Pairing Goals and Objectives with Learning Strengths

An Individualized Education Plan (IEP) is in each child's confidential folder. These reports and documents are prepared to inform all on how to work with and support the development of each child. Charting each child's IEP objectives provides a visual reference point of each child's present skill level and where her or his work may be heading.

Consider the benefit of incorporating both a child's strengths and his or her IEP objectives on the same chart. This would embed the IEP objectives within the strengths-based choices that each child makes throughout the day at school. As the child actively engages in interacting with peers, theorizing, and exploring materials and activities of interest, those strengths will drive the development of her or his objectives. Those working with Laura may observe her interest in dinosaurs and nature listed on the Strengths and Objectives chart and use this information to introduce positional concepts.

The Strengths and Objectives chart also serves as a reference for grouping children. Laura enjoys using dinosaurs in the sand table, which is filled with sand, pebbles, and pine tags, and the teacher may invite Hannah to join them in setting up a dinosaur habitat. The children may decide if they want the Ty-rannosaurus Rex in front of, behind, or on top of the pebbles. Depending on each child's present skill level, she may point to or name the position, front, behind, or on top, and then place the T-Rex in that location.

The added bonus is that data collected during these interactions and pe-riods of engagement also serves to inform each child's progress on her or his IEP objectives. Table 2.2 shows a sample chart of strengths and IEP objectives. On such a chart, each child's objectives are charted in sequential order, as well as the name or initials of every child who shares the same objective for the year.

Although it is efficient to create as many of the organizational systems as possible before the children arrive, it also is important to realize that form-ing systems is a process that will emerge and evolve with the children's work as well as your own intentions. As is necessary with establishing reciprocal communication with team members, continually refining your classroom sys-tems each year is another way to reflect upon and review their worth and effectiveness.

Creating Systems for Documenting and Organizing Each Child's Work

Documentation at the beginning of the school year will center on captur-ing the essence of each child. Plan now, before the year begins, to prepare documentation forms. The documentation may include photographing each child as she or he gains comfort in the new environment, chooses from the variety of materials available, and connects with others in the room. The doc-umentation might also include recording conversations by hand or with tape recorders. It will include hard copies, photocopies, or photographs of the work the children create. (See Chapter 3 for more on observations at the beginning of the year.)

Table 2.2. Child's Strengths and IEP Objectives

CONFIDENTIAL INFORMATION			Other children with same objectives
Child	Strengths	Objectives	
Laura	*Interests:* insects and dinosaurs *Intelligences:* Verbal/Linguistic Visual/Spatial Naturalist Intrapersonal	*Communication:* Demonstrate and name positional concepts: front/back, bottom/top, behind/in front of, etc. Demonstrate use of objects; given an oral description of an object's use, pointing to or naming object.	*Communication:* Harry Deborah David Ben

A form that has proven to be open to many uses and can be easily created before the children arrive is a simple class roster with each child's full name. Spaces can be included at the top of the page to write the topic of the list and the date. Multiple copies of this roster can be made available to use as needed. Such rosters can be used for noting whether children have brought in their supplies, spare clothes, and forms, or to note which types of documentation have been collected on each child during the first days of school. Table 2.3 shows a sample Roster Form.

Using the Roster Form on the first days allows those documenting to note which children have been photographed, which children's conversations have been recorded, and which types of work has been saved from each child. Abbreviations can be created for each notation that is made: for example, Ph = photo taken, C = conversation recorded, E/w = engaged with noted, Rw = representational work filed, and so on. As noted above, recording each child's name and the date on the pieces of documentation serves many purposes. Such details on the documentation allow for others to identify each child's work, and other children who are interested in this type of work, to be able to identify a friend for co-construction. Placing the name and date on children's work also allows the work to serve as authentic examples of data collection and to document individual progress.

The forms created for the first days of school might note the subtleties of what soothes, engages, and interests each child. The form might also include the date and duration of the engagement, which could serve as a baseline. The form might have a space to note which children interacted with others; who initiated, sustained, and closed the interaction; the mode of communication around the interaction; the preferred materials; and the type of interaction.

What about those empty bulletin boards that we typically decorate before the children arrive on that first day of school? The bulletin boards may welcome the children yet remain unfilled in anticipation of having the documentation of the children's first work grace their spaces. One year, Denise left a bulletin board empty even during the first weeks of school. She did not get any comments from the families during the orientation visit, from her colleagues, or even from her administration, but she wondered if they were puzzled by or maybe even looked disapprovingly at the empty board. She had planned to use the empty board to provoke ideas from the children. Realizing that she had not conveyed her teaching intentions to anyone except the teaching assistants, she specifically wrote about the provocation and eventually created a documentation board to share the process with the entire school community.

OH! WHAT AN EMPTY BULLETIN BOARD WILL INSPIRE

The simple act of leaving the bulletins boards in the classroom blank can have extraordinary results. Blank bulletins boards present an opportunity to get to know children's strengths at the beginning of the year. On one of the first days

Table 2.3. Roster Form

Date: 9/10/10

Topic of Checklist: Documentation of First Week

Person Completing Checklist: Jasmine Vaughn

Child's Name	Documentation	Child's Name	Documentation
Jess	Ph C, attached E/w: Jake, Mel Has not created Rw	Mel	Ph C, attached E/w: Dotty, Charlie, Jess Rw filed
April	Ph C, attached (PECS, gestures) E/w: Jake, Molly Rw filed	Max	Ph C, attached E/w: Material Rw filed
Charlie	Ph C, attached E/w: Dotty, Mel Has not created Rw	Molly	Ph C, attached E/w: April Rw filed
Jake	Ph C, attached (One word replies) E/w: Jess, April Rw filed	Dotty	Ph C, attached E/w: Charlie, Mel Rw filed

of the year, Denise's class gathered to plan what should go on the empty bulletin board in the classroom. The children sat with their clipboards and pencils, and started drawing what would be important to put on the empty board. The common thread in two of the children's plans was a river. Each child had experienced rivers with their families over the summer. Kelly had camped with her family at a river. She was very interested in the birds she had seen flying above the river. Michael had seen rocks, logs, and old tires in the James River. The group decided that they would make the James River on the board. Jamie decided to make waves, a child, and a sky for our river.

When the group next had a chance to meet, they developed a group plan for the river bulletin board. The children drew what they had experienced with their families and wanted to include on the plan for the board (see Figure 2.3).

Figure 2.3. James River Plan Drawing

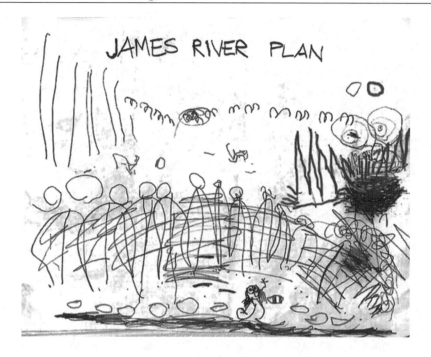

A larger group of interested children formed who used books to research clouds and skies before creating the skies over the James River. By reviewing the children's plans to represent the skies over the James River, the teachers were clear that they would have to offer a variety of art materials. Some children wanted to represent the puffiness of clouds and chose collage materials to create three-dimensional clouds. Other children focused on the colors of the sky on stormy and clear days. Two friends stood side by side at the easel and collaborated on the canvases for our James River skies.

Jamie wanted to replicate the exact color of purple in the photo of a sky that he chose to follow as a plan (see Figure 2.4). Jamie and Michael searched for that color throughout the supplies in our room. When Jamie did not find an exact color match, he had to dictate a note to ask other teachers, "Do you have a light-purple crayon?" Jamie delivered the note down the hall and showed Miss Debbie his photo. Together, they developed the color he needed by covering the marks from a purple oil pastel with a white one. Ready with his research and art materials, Jamie represented a sky for our James River bulletin board.

Another group met to research and draw plans for water birds. Kelly followed her plan and created a Kingfisher bird (see Figure 2.5). With all of the plans and materials that the groups made, they quickly ran out of room on the empty bulletin board in the class. The entire project process moved to the

Figure 2.4. Jamie Using Library Book to Draw a Sky

large bulletin board in the hallway (see Figure 2.6.). Everyone in the school community had access to the class's strengths-based interests and capabilities.

Since the children and their families, as well as the teachers, were all interested in rivers and river life, they expanded their collective interests and study by taking a trip to the Maymont Nature Center in nearby Richmond, Virginia. The children, families, teachers, and therapists enjoyed a morning of following their common interest.

**Figure 2.5. Kelly
Making Her
River Bird**

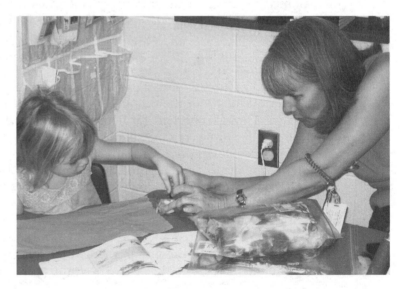

Figure 2.6. The Finished Bulletin Board

SUMMARY

As this story about an empty bulletin board shows, from the very beginning of the year, there lies hidden potential in leaving spaces in the classroom for children to grace with their strengths-based work. When education communities grant educators the necessary time and resources to forge relationships with families and begin to discover the strengths of the children, the year begins on a firm foundation based on strong relationships. By listening to and relying on families to teach us as educators about their children, we can launch relationships built on reciprocal communication and respect for the expertise of all. The invaluable information that families provide serves as springboards from which we can create systems to organize and use the strengths of each child. Learning from many of our families that spending time outdoors with nature was a passion of their children, Denise was able to facilitate this James River project and embed a broader band of the children's interests and their skill strengths to begin to meet their needs. This bulletin board attracted many people—drawing in students, parents, teachers, and even the larger school community as they gathered around the bulletin board that was created though the students' common interests.

CHAPTER 3

Getting Started:
The Vital Role of Observation
and Documentation

The beginning of the school year is a fresh start to a new year for most teachers. Rested from the summer and armed with new materials and books, a renewed look at the goals for the year, and, most important, new students to learn about, creates an excitement in the school environment. At the same time, it is a very stressful time of year. There is a multitude of paperwork to get through, preparation of the classroom environment, acquiring and organizing new materials, reading and organizing IEP objectives and goals, providing for specific accommodations, setting up service schedules, and getting to know and establish a relationship with new families in the classroom. It is easy to become overwhelmed and it can be difficult, at times, to focus on the true purpose for teaching—to learn about each child in order to best teach them. That is a tall order to fill, yet one that most teachers truly strive for despite all the distractions of daily responsibilities. How can we go about that task?

LEARNING ABOUT THE CHILDREN: OBSERVE, OBSERVE, OBSERVE

Bev Boss, a leader in the early childhood education community, emphasizes the importance of taking the time at the beginning of the year to step back and really observe each child in the classroom. These are clear and simple instructions, yet it actually takes a lot of courage to follow through. As stated above, there is an overwhelming number of things that must be done at the beginning of the year. As teachers look at each child's IEP, there are vast and widely varied levels of objectives to cover in the school year. Taking the time to observe the children in the class can feel like a risky venture, given this daunting task ahead of teachers. The teacher gene compels teachers to get themselves, the environment, the children, and the materials organized. Teachers feel anxious to get themes planned in order to insert objectives into the lesson plans, and this is a natural response to the chaos and stress at the beginning of the school year.

Yet, while the concept of being very planned out ahead of time can be comforting, it often causes teachers to focus on following the plan: making sure the activities are completed, the crafts are done (with each child doing each craft), a particular circle game is played (it does, after all, reinforce both counting and positional concepts), the finger-play is recited (reinforcing body parts, colors), and so forth. Yet, in the meantime, what are we actually learning about who the children are, as individuals, in that initial time period? (Sussna, 2000). Reading children's IEPs provides some information about the child's challenges, but does not particularly provide information or insight as to how to best reach each child. Carter, Cividanes, Curtis, and Lebo (2010, p. 18) share that a teacher can "turn to the many resources available to learn about guidance techniques or use a published curriculum to help with planning. But to truly share meaningful experiences with children your must learn to become a reflective teacher." In order to reflect on children's experiences it is vital to take the time to observe those same children.

Taking Time to Observe

Debbie began the school year with her plans, activities, songs, and so forth intact as usual. But this year, she began the process of spending more time observing the children. As a result, she began to glean information about her students much earlier in the year than usual: Ellie was like the princess in the princess and the pea story—she couldn't sit still if a pile of goose-down mattresses were supporting her. Ian did not like any craft activity and would throw tantrums every time the class sat down to complete one. Amani was a puzzle to be solved. He was at times very uncooperative about changing centers when it was time to rotate, and Debbie had to brace herself for the tornado of emotion that would be expressed by him when the transition was made. At other times, however, he was not as bothered about the changes. There didn't seem to be any consistent factor in his acceptance of center changes. He might balk in leaving a center today and be content to change from that same center the next day. In addition, there was no one center that seemed to elicit these responses consistently. Debbie was aware that this child was on the autism spectrum and that changes and transitions might be difficult for him, so she had provided him with visual reinforcements in the form of a visual schedule and pictures depicting what would happen next. He continued, however, to demonstrate this inconsistent resistance to changing centers.

As a result of this more in-depth observation process, Debbie began to realize that understanding what was responsible for these children's behaviors, interests, and motivations might be a more valuable tool than her well-planned lessons. At that point Debbie stepped back and made what felt like a precarious decision; she was going to let go of her agenda for a while and really spend some time finding out who these children were.

Yikes! That being said, there needs to be some clarification about what that means and what it does not mean. It does not mean Debbie was about to encourage anarchy in the classroom! It did not mean that there would not be planning or structure or routines in the classroom. As ECSE (early childhood special education) teachers know, structure and routine are very important for this age group. But it did mean letting go of Debbie's own thoughts and plans as to which themes would be presented and when they would be presented to a certain degree, and becoming more child-centered in her thinking and teaching.

In thinking about how to go about providing more time and structure for the observation process, Debbie decided to keep the basic structure and support in the classroom—including visual schedules and supports—and decided to make plans around the routines of the day. However, rather than planning around a particular theme that created pressure to produce particular products on a particular time line, Debbie decided to begin the year with more process-oriented activities and crafts that were flexible in scope and offered a variety of options for how each child would participate in each activity.

It was also decided that while there would be a limit on the number of children in a center, the adults in the classroom would not dictate to children which center they should play in or how much time they should spend in that center (Casey & McWilliam, 2005; DiCarlo & Vagianos, 2009). Of course, an exception would be made to this rule if children were merely running from one center to another. That type of behavior indicates that a child is not self-regulated and needs boundaries in order to become regulated. A child who was running from one center to another was only providing adults with the information that the child was unfocused, and that information can be gleaned in very little time!

Informing Families

In preparation for this new style of teaching, a letter was written to the families of the children in the class explaining the reasoning behind the extent of time being provided for observation of their children's natural interests and behaviors. This communication ensured that the families would not have the same expectation of the amount of typical preschool art projects, as well as other products associated with teacher-planned activities and craft projects as their children began the new school year.

Beginning the Observation Process

Debbie began this process by creating a time-sampling observation chart that was functional for her classroom environment (see Appendix C). This form provides two key pieces of information: a quick check on a regular basis to see where children were playing and what materials they were using (DiCarlo & Vagianos, 2009), as well as an area for more detailed observations. Debbie soon found that this open-ended, process-oriented style of teaching provided an unexpected benefit: extra time to be with the children and play on a one-on-one basis rather than spending time managing planned activities!

After the initial self-doubts and anxiety, Debbie was excited and amazed at what she was learning—so early in the school year!—about these children who were in her care. Ellie (the "princess and the pea" child) was constantly seeking proprioceptive input and, given her choice, would engage in activities that provided sensory stimulation and pressure for comfort, such as playing in the sensory table, wrapping herself in the bean bag chair, playing on the Sit-and-Spin, swinging, even getting inside the netted bag that held the playground balls (DiCarlo & Vagianos, 2009)! Ian was very competent at gross motor activities and liked using construction materials and problem-solving with large-piece puzzles, but he definitely shied away from activities involving fine motor skills. Even though this was not included in his IEP coming into the school year, Debbie's observations revealed that he was, in fact, fairly weak in using or working with his hands and had very limited skills in fine motor activities (DiCarlo & Vagianos, 2009).

As Debbie observed Amani, she came to realize the source of his issues with moving from one center to another. Amani did have difficulty with transitions, as she had expected. However, Debbie also discovered that he really liked anything that had anything to do with vehicles, animals, or dinosaurs. She began to realize that if Amani was being asked to leave the block center and the animals were out in that area, he would have a tantrum. If the above items were not present in that center that day, he was more amicable to changing centers, perhaps anticipating that the table toys might have a dinosaur puzzle or housekeeping would have animals that day. The type of center did not matter; it was more important that those areas of interest (vehicles, animals, dinosaurs) were in some way represented. That information went a long way toward helping Amani experiment with new materials and transitions more readily in the classroom (DiCarlo & Vagianos, 2009).

Learning such in-depth information about the children in a short period of time certainly confirmed the validity of taking the time to observe, and Debbie eagerly went about the task of learning how to implement these strategies. However, teacher doubt reared its ugly head again when it was suggested to Debbie that children had to be pushed to explore multiple centers and modes of play. Debbie once again took a deep breath and decided to trust her intuitive sense that this process was worth providing the time and freedom for free exploration. Debbie had every intention to challenge the children to move beyond their areas of comfort and familiarity in their play; however, she gave herself permission to spend some time just trying to understand which of their interests and strengths led them to their choices in play.

This approach also helped her in identifying which areas and activities the children avoided as well as why they might be avoiding them. In providing the children with the freedom to make their own choices, Debbie was able to observe more than just interests, strengths, and challenges. She was also provided with a natural opportunity to look at each child's individual personality and temperament in more depth and to decide how to support those differences (Pelco & Reed-Victor, 2003). Debbie began asking such questions as: Is the child extroverted or introverted? Shy or very outgoing? Methodical in problem-solving or intuitive? Does the child follow through with choices naturally or need extra encouragement to do so? What seems to be this child's learning style? Does this child learn verbally, by hearing information; visually, through actually seeing something done; or tactilely, by actually doing? Is she best reached through movement, music, literature, art, nature; and does she work best in groups or alone? Early in the school year, the observations resulting from these questions took Debbie's introduction to each child far beyond what she had learned from the families and read in their confidential folders.

An Observation Checklist

A more in-depth look at observation provides teachers with some guidelines as to how to carry out this process. Bertrand and Cebula (1980, cited in Grace, 1992, p. 3) clarify, "During systematic observation, young children should be observed when they are playing alone, in small groups, at various times of day and in various circumstances. Systematic observation must be objective, selective, unobtrusive and carefully recorded."

How does the teacher record such information while at the same time trying to teach the children the many new roles, routines, and structures of the day that must be learned at the beginning of the year? Some suggestions that might be helpful in this regard are: placing sticky notes or index cards strategically throughout the room so that any adult can record an observation, taking pictures of the children to record their activity (pictures as documentation will be discussed later in this chapter), small notebooks placed in different centers for adults to write observations, and clipboards that contain checklists such as the one in Appendix D are valuable resources in gathering such information in a systematic manner. For more skill-related observations, a chart such as the one in Appendix E can be used. In addition, the roster checklist in Chapter 2 can be used to provide and record valuable information about the children from the first days of school. In the appendixes you will find additional forms to use for observation and documentation.

SUPPORTING THE PROCESS OF OBSERVATION

How do you make time for these observations? There are many possibilities to get help in this process. This section will mention a few, and that will inevitably spark your creative process that will aid you in coming up with additional scenarios that suit your situation.

Instructional Assistants: A Valuable Resource

It is the authors' opinion that instructional assistants in our school systems are a much underappreciated and underestimated group of professionals whose work with teachers and children is a valuable asset on a daily basis. "There is no dispute that paraprofessionals are an integral part of the educational landscape. Nowhere is the critical role of paraprofessionals more evident than in general education classes where students with disabilities are being included with classmates who do not have disabilities" (Broer, Edelman, & Giangreco, 2001, p. 485). Yet, many teachers continue to think of the instructional assistants with whom they work as someone to make copies or put up bulletin boards, which is disrespectful of the many abilities that they possess and also diminishes the effectiveness of the educational team in the classroom. It is tremendously beneficial to seek the judgment and perspective of the instructional assistants with whom you work as well as other teachers and therapists.

Generally, instructional assistants spend approximately the same amount of time with the children as the teacher and therefore have many opportunities to observe children. Although the final responsibility for assessment lies with the teacher, many instructional assistants have learned quite a bit about child development as a result of spending a good amount of time with young children. In addition, free from the final responsibility of the class as a whole, an instructional assistant may actually be more adept at taking a step back and noting behaviors or interests that teachers may very well have missed. In Figures 3.1 and 3.2, Miss Judy and Miss Susan, both instructional assistants with their own unique strengths and interests, provide scaffolding for students to create a real tree house, and explore with Gavin how to create a zip line from the tree house in order to move the play figures in a box that became an elevator.

Figure 3.1. Miss Judy Facilitates Children as They Create a "Tree House"

Figure 3.2. Miss Susan Scaffolds Gavin's Problem-Solving Skills as He Creates a Zip Line for the Tree House

If these two talented people had not been afforded the ability to interact with and become an integral part of the teaching and observation process, these opportunities would have been lost.

As both teachers and instructional assistants observe the children, it is important for all adults in the classroom to take the time to discuss what they have observed. This can be done at formal sessions, in the classroom while setting up in the morning, at the end of the day, or at rest time. When is not as important as just taking the opportunity to collaboratively examine who the child is based on information that has been gathered. It is inevitable that certain adults will notice things that others might overlook, and it is beneficial to make use of those different perspectives in the documentation process.

There is also a need for adult classroom management to keep the flow of the classroom productive, engaging, and smooth while observation of the children is taking place. When setting up a scenario for observation it is important to establish roles of the adults in the room. While all adults can certainly grab one of the handy lists that you have placed around the room and document their observation of skills, interests, and so forth, as they are evidenced throughout the day, there should be a designated observer and a designated classroom manager. This delegation of roles helps adults know who will be primarily responsible for maintaining order and engagement in the classroom and who will be primarily responsible for observation of the children (Broer, Edelman, & Giangreco, 2001).

Creating an Optimal Child-to-Adult Ratio

There are many ways to provide a better adult-to-child ratio in those early days of school.

Phasing Children Into the Start of the School Year. Consider creating a phase-in system for your class if your school system will allow it. A phase-in schedule allows for maximum staff-child ratio so that there are more adults to handle the transitory process of beginning school and to initially observe the children. With extra adults facilitating this process, children learn the routine and how to take care of personal belongings in a shorter period of time, which will provide you with more observation time in the future. Most administrators are more likely to approve a new system if you create a proposal that is outlined in a way that demonstrates the rationale, process, and the outcome. One option to consider is to create a rotating schedule for the ECSE classes. Ask your administrator if you can create a rotating schedule for the beginning of school so that only one class begins at a time, with each class having 2 days of school in the phase-in schedule. (For example: Class A attends Monday and Wednesday, Class B attends Tuesday and Thursday.) The teachers from the class not in school on a given day serve as extra adults in the classroom, helping children and observing their interests, strengths, and needs. Another option is to create a rotating schedule for your own class so that only half of the children in the class attend school at one time for the first week.

Collaborating with Therapists. Work with therapists to create as much collaborative time to work with the children in the classroom as possible; they may even be able to increase their time or send in assistants for those first few weeks of school (Carnahan, Williamson, Clarke, & Sorensen, 2009). In addition, most school systems have some kind of program in the high school for students interested in becoming teachers. You could plan ahead with coordinators at the high school level to explore the possibility of providing assistance in your classroom during the school year. This plan would both provide the high school students with experience and you with additional help in your classroom

Accessing Parents. Plan a parent swap between two or more preschool classes in your school in order to access parent volunteers. Ask parents to volunteer at the beginning of the year, and schedule them to be in another teacher's class while you utilize a parent from his or her room. This allows for extra help without creating a problem of a child being distressed with his or her parent in the room.

Asking for Volunteers. Finally, look around for available volunteers in your school and community. You might be surprised at how many people would be willing to come in and help out for a day or 2 (or 3) at the beginning of the year. Some people to consider contacting might be teachers who have recently retired, members of your school's parent–teacher organization, people who substitute during the school year whom you have developed a relationship with in the past, or just people you know from the community who work well with children. Of course, in most school systems you will need to plan ahead for this opportunity, as the local school administration or school board may need to approve those individuals to work in your room.

Creating an Environment Conducive to Observation

As the new school year begins it is crucial to consider the actual classroom environment and how it will be structured. In considering your environment it is again important to remember to be flexible as the year goes on, as different groups of children may have different needs.

Setting Up the Physical Environment. In any preschool classroom there are some basic areas of play that represent the primary developmental domains and interest areas of young children and provide opportunities for exploration, skill development, discovery, and creativity, such as: Science/Nature, Blocks, Housekeeping/Dramatic Play, Table Toys or a Manipulative area, Sensory Tables or areas, Book area, Art area, Computer area, and an Outside area, (Dodge, Colker, & Heroman, 2002). One of many valuable resources for those who are beginning teaching is *The Creative Curriculum for Preschool* (Dodge et al., 2002), as it provides a vast amount of information about setting up a workable classroom and guidelines for setting up interest areas in the classroom. The difference in setting up an environment for observation, however, will be the manner in which these areas are programmed to enable children to move toward interest areas while at the same time providing teachers and instructional assistants additional opportunities to observe.

The manner in which the classroom is arranged around center areas is vital to beginning the year with the classroom as the third teacher. The way in which furniture is arranged may also serve to define areas for small-group play, which lends itself to more engagement of the children with materials and one another. Organizing the room so adults can see as much as possible from every location both ensures children's safety and allows adults more freedom to observe.

Choosing Materials. It is generally known that the aforementioned areas would be made available to the children in an early childhood classroom (Ganz & Flores, 2010). The key to creating a self-sustaining environment, however, is to present materials that require the minimum amount of adult assistance yet sustain an engaging and calm level of play and interaction, especially at the beginning of the year. Providing materials that fall into the independent range of functioning for the majority of the children in the room reduces the need for physical assistance and keeps low the level of the children's frustration. There will, of course, still be quite enough for the teacher to facilitate, such as learning the new routine, self-help skills, and social negotiations. The goal is to keep such needs at a minimum to provide the adults with more time for the observation process. For example, art materials would be provided, but no actual teacher-determined product would be required.

The manipulatives and puzzles that are chosen should be simple so that children are able to use them independently or with the help of a peer. The materials in the room (and in particular, in the dramatic play area) should be set up so that they are easily approached and accessed and children have a limited range of materials available. This limitation of materials reduces the amount of materials to be managed, allows for a gradual increase of materials so the class has time to learn how to use the materials appropriately and discover where those materials belong (i.e., Is this particular material restricted to one particular center?), and provides children the opportunity to learn how to properly take care of and clean up the materials. This attention to the specifics of how materials are introduced and used may sound as if it conflicts with our vision of child-centered learning; however, providing children with careful information and structure regarding the use of materials presented is essential to the process of child-centered learning. Such careful structuring at the start of the year eventually allows the children to have more independence and, therefore, gives the adults more freedom and time to observe and interact with the children. In addition, because it is the beginning of the year, all the materials in this particular environment will create a novel experience for the children, decreasing the need for large numbers of materials to keep the children's interest.

Open-Ended Activities. The use of open-ended activities to begin the school year is beneficial to the observation process in multiple ways:

1. Open-ended activities require less time for overall planning, freeing up time for the teacher to observe and document those observations.
2. Open-ended activities allow teachers to observe children's learning styles, preferences, and interests, as well as those areas they tend to avoid. Does the child tend to navigate toward play with manipulatives, block-building and design, puzzles, categorization of materials, or more dramatic play? Does the natural world of animals, insects, and materials such as shells, rocks, and wood initially attract her attention? Does she gravitate toward: Music? Math-related materials? Literacy-related materials? Active (kinesthetic) play? Visual arts or sensory experiences?
3. Open-ended activities allow for multiple opportunities to observe children's social levels, personalities, behavioral tendencies, and degree of playfulness. Does the child tend to play alone or with others? Is she a leader or follower? Introverted or extroverted? What kind of social negotiation skills does the child have? Which areas of social interactions are strongest, and which create challenges?

Some examples of open-ended materials and activities for the beginning of the year might include:

- Play dough: This is an effective material with which to begin the year. It provides sensory input and requires little adult attention. As an observation tool, it allows the teacher to observe certain skills and preferences. Some children may be sensitive to the feeling of play dough on their hands, a clue for the teacher that there may be some tactile sensitivity.
- Sensory activities, such as sand tables, bean tables, water tables, etc.: Use of a sensory area such as an indoor sandbox provides teachers with information about the children. Does the child seem to crave the sensory stimulation? What kind of activity is she involved in? For the children, the additional sensory input helps with the adjustment of a new environment.
- Open-ended art materials can be provided for exploration rather than product-oriented projects, such as collage materials, different types of paints and paper, wire, clay, hole punchers, pastels, etc.
- Limited number of blocks paired with animals or cars.
- Self-sustaining manipulatives such as peg boards, lacing cards, magnet blocks, etc.
- Nature-related themes set up for dramatic play: A farm, forest, or jungle habitat. Natural materials will especially appeal to those children with a "natural intelligence."
- Housekeeping set up with limited materials to ensure easy cleanup.

These are just some suggestions; whatever activities you choose to begin the school year with, the challenge is to create as many opportunities as you can for observing the children with as little adult facilitation as possible.

Creating Lesson Plans to Support Observation. Now that you have planned for extra adult support and looked at the environment and the routine of the day, the next step is to create daily plans. These plans should be developed in a manner that will allow you the freedom and flexibility to observe the children while, at the same time, making available activities and materials that will provide you with as much information as possible about the children in your room. Probably the most important word here is flexibility. As the school year is just beginning and there are new students to learn about, it is most important to give yourself and the children permission to "go with the flow." Rather than creating plans that include specific art projects or center activities, provide multiple materials and experiences in your environment and take a step back to see how the children interact with the environment and with one another throughout the daily schedule. While a loosely based plan of centers or activities may be necessary, these plans should be fluid and flexible in order to flow with the children's interests.

As an aid for flexible planning, attach small sticky notes to your lesson plan for that day or week, especially at the beginning of the year. Activities, books, songs, and so forth listed on individual notes can be moved around during the course of a day or to different days if activities planned do not mesh well with what is happening in the classroom. Some sticky notes may very well end up in the trash can or in a file for another year; both are perfectly valid destinations at times, when the activity does not suit a particular group of children. Another way to stay fluid in planning is to create lesson plans on the computer, with a limited amount of planning for the end of the week, in order to follow the children's interest as the week progresses. (Chapter 7 provides a sample lesson plan.)

Taking Observation Further: Using Photographs to Inform

Teachers at The Sabot School came to realize the tremendous power of using pictures as a source of documentation (Carter et al., 2010; Morrison, 1999; Vakil, Freeman, & Swim, 2003). Using pictures as a means of documenting the children is a valuable tool in many respects. Pictures taken by an assigned photographer in those beginning days provide the teacher with a viewpoint of a child in contexts that might have been missed while engaged with other children. Pictures provide literal snapshots of the children in the learning process across developmental domains. Children at play provide teachers with information regarding interaction with peers and individual levels of playfulness as they interact in the housekeeping center. The children might be problem-solving and planning as they build in the block area, showing initiative and follow through as they play with puzzles and table toys, using fine motor skills as they play with manipulatives, and collaborating with peers as they work together on an art project to make an airplane or rocket ship in the art area. These examples are, of course, just a sampling of the information that can be gathered through the use of pictures as one tool of documentation (Vakil et al., 2003).

Figures 3.3 and 3.4 show Parker learning to create a ramp by watching Wesley. This interaction provided quite a bit of information to Parker's team, even though the original intent of the photo documentation was to capture Wesley's problem-solving! These pictures demonstrate that Parker was interested enough in cars and their propulsion to remain in one place and learn from observation, that Parker had reached the cognitive level of beginning problem-solving, and that peer modeling was obviously an effective tool for teaching Parker new skills. This was quite a revelation, and the information was used to provide Parker with additional opportunities for skill and language development using vehicles as a medium to promote interest in those activities. Figure 3.5 demonstrates Parker's first motivated attempt to cut on a line.

Attempts to encourage Parker to move from fringing to cutting on a line had proved frustrating for all involved, including Parker. The incentive to stay focused on both the task of cutting and the effort of tracking the line just wasn't there for him—until he had the opportunity to create a train out of those straight lines. Bingo! What a difference! The information gathered the year before about his interest in vehicles was continuing to reinforce Parker's skill development.

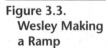
**Figure 3.3.
Wesley Making
a Ramp**

**Figure 3.4.
Parker Making
a Ramp**

FROM OBSERVATION TO DOCUMENTATION

The process of observing the children in such an extensive manner leads naturally to the gathering of authentic data for assessment and planning purposes throughout the year. Helm, Beneke, and Steinheimer reflect on the benefit of using documentation:

> The school visitor was able to see what children were learning because teachers had carefully collected, analyzed, interpreted, and displayed the evidence of learning. This use of documentation is directly related to what research in the early childhood field has shown about how children learn. (2007, p. 7)

Figure 3.5. Parker Cutting To Make His Favorite: A Train!

The use of documentation provides a continuous flow of information as the school year progresses.

Documentation as the School Year Begins

The first pieces of documentation at the beginning of the year have multiple purposes: Documentation provides families with a snapshot of the child's day; others in the school environment come to know the children; and teachers are provided an authentic baseline of the children's development, skills, and concept knowledge. The old saying, "A picture is worth a thousand words" is an understatement when associated with the general relief parents feel when they are actually able to see with their own eyes that their child is engaged and playing and smiling in his new environment.

Documentation as a Means of Authentic Assessment

Occasionally, a child will not be engaged or happy. Although it is more difficult to see as a teacher or a parent, it also does provide important information. Children who have difficulty adjusting to new environments challenge teachers to provide provocations to which the children can connect and that will serve as catalysts for the children's connections with others. In our practice, children who presented such challenges afforded us the opportunity to rethink and to introduce such children into the environment in a manner that best suits the children's strengths and personality. The following story is a composite of many children with whom Debbie and Denise have worked with in the past.

Juanita's Story

One student, Juanita, was painfully shy and reserved coming into the classroom. She most definitely did not want to leave the safe confines of home and Mom and branch out to the rest of the world. While Juanita did not cry or throw a tantrum (she was much too controlled for that), she also absolutely refused to become part of the class in any way. Juanita was coming into the classroom, stopping right inside the door, and covering her eyes with her hands. (In order, it seemed, to negate other people's very existence!) She was one of those children who did not seek or want to be comforted by new adults until she developed a comfort level of her own. Children such as Juanita are sometimes more of a challenge than those who will yell and scream and want to be held. How do teachers help children like Juanita who do not want help from others? With Juanita, Debbie decided to back off and observe her, just as she was observing other children's strengths and interests. Debbie didn't feel comfortable letting a child be "on her own," so to speak, even if it was her choice. How could Debbie let her just stand there with her hands over her eyes, not participating in any way with the class? What would Debbie tell Juanita's mom and dad when they asked how she was doing that day? But Debbie decided to let Juanita lead her rather than the other way around. Of course, Debbie continued to invite Juanita to join the class, but Juanita did not answer. After a short time, however, her hands came down and she felt brave enough to see everyone in the classroom. From information Debbie had gleaned from Juanita's mom before school, she knew that books were one of Juanita's interests. For a few days, Debbie began to leave books on the shelf beside her; then Debbie moved them into the book corner, which, luckily, was not far away. Juanita began to go into the book corner and seemed very happy to be by herself looking at books.

Debbie's challenge, of course, was discovering how to make Juanita comfortable around the other children and getting Juanita out of the book corner. Again, the combination of information provided by her parents and Debbie's observations of Juanita, as well as other children in the room, made an incredible difference in how Debbie managed this situation. In situations like this, Debbie and her instructional assistant, Robyn, would look for other children in the class who seemed more comfortable socially and had similar interests to a child who was more reticent to join in play. Two children in the class, Charlene and Lisa, exhibited many of the same interests as Juanita. They would pretend to be wild animals with baby cubs one minute, then "real" mommies feeding (or saving) their own babies the next! However, while Charlene and Lisa were acting these interests out in dramatic play, Juanita was looking at books. Debbie decided that if she could not get Juanita to leave the book area to go to dramatic play, the dramatic play area would need to come to Juanita! Debbie and Robyn began to put book and dramatic play items together. The best baby dolls, a doctor kit, animal puppets, and so forth were placed in the book corner, along with books that related to those subjects. The other children, particularly these outgoing young girls, Charlene and Lisa, were drawn to the area to use those materials. The rule was that the materials had to stay in that area. At first Juanita would turn her back away from the other children. But it only took a day or so for her interests to win out, and Juanita began to join in the play, timidly at first, but her comfort level with these peers who had come to her soon increased!

Some educators might question this decision, perhaps feeling that Debbie might have been feeding into Juanita's unwillingness to join into the classroom activities. However, to Debbie, Juanita's reluctance was not so much an unwillingness as it was an integral part of who this child was. Respecting that about her personality and accommodating it as a need, rather than forcing her to join in despite her level of discomfort, seemed to Debbie a more thoughtful and productive route to go.

Debbie did move the materials back to the dramatic play area after she felt that Juanita had reached a level of comfort with the other children, which happened within a short period of time. Within a day Juanita had timidly moved to the housekeeping center. At first she sat in one particular seat at the table and played in a more parallel way, doing her own thing alongside the other children at the table. Soon, however, she branched out to associative play, playing with the same materials in the same manner but not really talking to or planning cooperatively with the other children playing. Within 2 weeks' time, Juanita was not only playing in a cooperative manner, she was actually initiating play scenarios and attempting to manage other children in the room!

Debbie made an amazing discovery about children who often display such reticence in joining into a new environment in the process. Often the driving force of self-imposed isolation is a need to feel in control of the environment. Once Juanita felt that control, her true temperament surfaced; this was a very competent child with definite ideas about how things should happen. Her actual challenge was not so much shyness but an inability to feel comfortable in an environment in which she did not feel in control. This changed Debbie's intentions as her teacher, and the objective became to help Juanita learn how to feel comfortable in social situations in which she did not have control to the extent she required. This entailed helping Juanita learn to negotiate with her peers and providing Juanita the opportunities and adult support needed for her to become flexible. This support enabled her to branch out in her play, expand her play environments, and engage with different peers in the classroom.

Creating Intentional Learners Through Observation and Documentation

Information gleaned from taking the time to observe children in the beginning of the year is invaluable in providing opportunities in which children become intentional learners. Children become active participants who are invested in their own learning process, rather than vessels that we try to fill with the information that is dictated by their IEP without the needed relevance that creates intentionality for the child (Odom, 2000; Sussna, 2000). The process of spending time observing and learning about children is evidenced in the story of "Is Miss Stephanie a Pirate?" that was described in Chapter 1. This project developed at the beginning of the year, when Debbie had loosely planned around the natural happenings in the environment at that time of year: apples, leaves, and so forth. Observing Brent, the child who had raised the question of whether Miss Stephanie was a pirate, provided Debbie with valuable information about this child. He was bright, inquisitive, funny, and creative. He was also, however, a very active child who needed some help with self-regulation. He was very set in his own idea of how to play with certain materials and had a difficult time working in a cooperative manner within a group. Because she had taken the time to really observe and get to know this young man, Debbie understood that this type of project would be beneficial to him as well as to the other members of the class in so many ways. Brent would benefit from being a part of a larger group in which group planning and decision making was crucial to the project, and he would be invested in the project, which naturally provided him with the internal drive to self-regulate in order to be part of something he was so eager to explore. In addition, his own qualities of creativity and intelligence were a driving force in the project and acted as models for the other children, and created opportunities for language development and skill-building within the classroom. This observation of Brent also required that Debbie become aware of where he was in his level of social interactions and play. Appendix E provides a time sampling chart for documenting children's level of play during the documentation process, not only at the beginning of the year but throughout the year.

The information gleaned from such observations helps in planning small groups—for example, in deciding which child might help Juanita move from parallel play to associative play. Who can work with Brent to encourage him to proceed to a more cooperative level of play?

This is a shift in thinking, from "filling the vessel" or attempting to "fill" the heads of the children with information that comes from a teacher-directed agenda to providing opportunities for the children to become invested in the process of learning themselves. However, this process requires that we provide ourselves with the permission to take the time to observe these children in order to judge what will capture their interest and imagination (Ganz & Flores, 2010; Koplow, 2007).

As Debbie proceeded in developing this style of observing children in order to get to know them, she became more and more comfortable with the time she was taking for such observation and extended the observation process to include checklists of skills.

USE OF DOCUMENTATION TO DETERMINE SKILLS AND CONCEPT KNOWLEDGE

Although it may seem redundant to observe for skills, since many are already listed on the child's IEP, these observation checklists can provide teachers with quite a bit of information about the children, aside from the information on the IEP (a sample of an IEP is presented in Chapter 7). Why is that? First of all, most IEPs are written in May, prior to the next school year, which generally begins in late August or early September. Early childhood educators are working with young children, and they can develop (or regress) quite a bit over the course of 3 to 4 months. So these checklists first and foremost provide current information. Also, information provided by the child's IEP does not necessarily provide teachers with the needed information about the style of learning or level of skill development of a particular child. A checklist of skills can provide the teacher with a quick glance at each child's level of development, as well as providing space to note specific observations on how that child is attempting mastery. In addition, a matrix of children's objectives (see Appendixes F and E) can be kept handy in order to remind those working with the children how they can insert those objectives into the play and explorations of the children, and to help adults keep data on the children as they observe them. These checklists can be housed in the areas specific to the skills in order to provide a means for anyone who is working with a child to quickly note the child's level of skill development. While we have provided two different checklists, these samples can be changed to accommodate any skill about which a teacher may want more information.

OBSERVING TO DOCUMENT SOCIAL/EMOTIONAL AND ADAPTIVE ABILITIES

Observation of children doesn't stop at concept knowledge or skills, however. Observations also help us to understand children's ability to self-regulate their sensory needs (Pelco & Reed-Victor, 2001; Reebye & Stalker, 2008) and their unique temperaments. Observations also provide information about children's ability to follow through with ideas and engagement and follow sequencing and directions, as well as their activity level, and so forth. While it may sound simplistic to remind teachers to look for these qualities in a specific manner, it is surprising how much more information teachers are able to collect about children by taking time to observe and watch for these specifics. For example, a teacher may find out that Alan has a difficult time following directions unless he is also able to see some visual representation of that information, or Diane may become very active when she is hungry or tired. Sure, most of us figure that out eventually throughout the year, but what a great way to gain insight about young children from the start! Such insights could actually prevent negative behaviors, as teachers are able to anticipate problems earlier and therefore help the children to make different choices as those situations come about.

Using Portfolios to Document and Assess

One method for organizing each child's work is to create a portfolio. Portfolios inform all who work with the children, from the teachers to the instructional assistant to the therapists to the families. Portfolios are, in essence, a compilation of the children's work, ideas, interests, strengths, imagination, knowledge, and skill and concept development. When teachers use documentation in an ongoing and engaging manner they are able to individualize curriculum to meet the needs of each child as an individual (Harris & Gleim, 2008). The compilation of information that constitutes a portfolio will also serve to demonstrate to others how the child is able to interact with others in his or her environment, whether it be social-emotionally or the ability to negotiate, collaborate, and communicate. Helm (2008) sums up the importance of documentation thusly:

> The use of observation notes and photographs, plus the collection of children's work, enables the teacher to be sure that anticipated learning becomes actual learning, that children master knowledge and skills, and that each individual child is participating in some way and moving toward the required curriculum goals or standards. (p. 8; see also Helm & Beneke, 2003; Helm, Beneke, & Steinheimer, 2007)

What Goes Into a Portfolio?

What will be included in the portfolio? (Arter & Spandel, 1991, as cited in Grace, Shores, & Brown, 1991) define the portfolio as a purposeful collection of student work that exhibits to the child and others his or her efforts or achievements in one or more areas.

Some examples of items that might be included in the portfolio include: pictures of the children working in centers and demonstrating their level of development, their skill level, their problem-solving abilities, and so forth. Conversations that children engage in among themselves and with teachers can be documented and included, either as transcripts or recordings. Children's actual work samples and art should be included, or pictures can be taken of such work so that the children are able to share their work at home with their families. Children's story ideas can be dictated to adults and included in the portfolio. In addition, checklists of skills, ongoing assessments (both informal and formal), and anecdotal records written by the various adults that work with the children should be a part of the portfolio.

In order to achieve the best understanding of the child as a whole, teachers will need to share with others in the school's environment the purpose and process of setting up the portfolio. In this way, all adults working with the children are able to see an opportunity to demonstrate an aspect of each child through the portfolio as a natural process of the day.

Gathering Materials. An example of how the materials gathered in a child's portfolio can inform adults as to how children learn and express their strengths comes from Debbie's own daughter, Hannah. Hannah had always had a fascination with animals, and this interest, along with her ability to play and think in an abstract manner and her natural intelligence, had become a known strength for Hannah during her time at Sabot School. Hannah was provided the opportunity to capitalize on her interests and strengths in her early years as her teacher, Marty, included her in outings to the woods, where she was able to make maps, inform other children about animals, and be a part of a group that theorized and shared ideas about how a tree might have fallen in the woods. Hannah's play often involved animals as she included many different children in her play scenarios. Hannah soon became known as a master player.

Hannah did not, however, demonstrate "normal" development in her early years. Hannah was not able to retain the academic information that was thought to be typical for kindergarten readiness. Hannah also had challenges with paying attention, unless it was a high-interest topic for her.

When it was time to enter kindergarten and take the pre-kindergarten screenings, Hannah was not able to name all the shapes, did not know many numbers, and had little knowledge of letter formation, although she had certainly been exposed to all of that information during her time at Sabot. When Hannah was asked to draw a person, she certainly did not meet the typical expectation of drawing a person with five or more recognizable features. However, from Hannah's portfolio from Sabot, Debbie was aware that she was able to draw an elephant in its entirety, with great detail, in a three-dimensional drawing! Debbie was also able to see from Hannah's contributions to the forest projects and in the dialogues around her play that this little girl, whatever her challenges, was a bright and competent child.

After a few months of kindergarten it became clear to Hannah's parents and her teacher that something was unusual about this little girl and that she would benefit from further testing. At the same time, Debbie took Hannah out of kindergarten, which was making her feel defeated, and put her back into pre-K at Sabot, in Irene's capable hands. It was a difficult decision to take Hannah out of kindergarten, but Hannah looked at Debbie one day and said, with tears rolling down her cheeks, "I want to go back to my old school. I was smart there." And Hannah was correct in this understanding. Hannah's portfolio held so many examples of her "smarts" that it was clear to Debbie that there was something specific going on with Hannah's learning.

When Hannah returned to pre-K at Sabot her interests and strengths were again utilized as a means to further her skills. During this time Hannah used her symbolic thinking to create personas for letters and numbers and had them attend a Number and Letter Party, which was included in her portfolio. (See Figure 3.6.)

Creating these personas helped Hannah to connect to and therefore memorize the letters and numbers, a skill she would use many times in her school career. As Hannah aged, she shared that she had come to the realization that

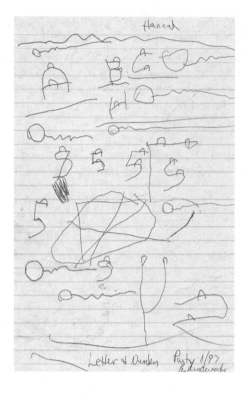

Figure 3.6. Hannah's Number and Letter Party

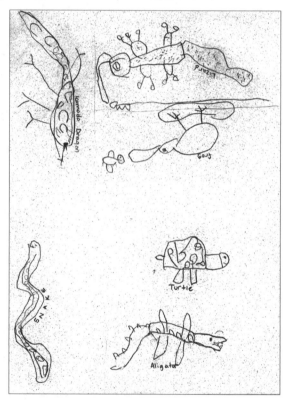

Figure 3.7. The Best Animals Ever

she could draw on this skill of making meaningful connections in order to memorize more rote information.

Hannah also began to draw some of her favorite animals in more depth, which seemed to make her more aware of the characteristics of people. Her drawings became more and more sophisticated during that time. (See Figure 3.7.)

After an extensive exploration of bicycles with a parent who had volunteered to work with these 5-year-olds, who were experiencing the joy of learning to ride a two-wheeler, Hannah completed a very detailed picture of herself on a bike (see Figure 3.8), with an explanation of how it works.

Figure 3.8. The Bicycle Project

This is my little bell. This is me riding in my helmet. There are my little streamers. And the pedals. And these are butterflies and my basket. You take your hands and hold onto the little bars and then you take your foot on the two pedals. And then you start like running, but the bike is moving, not you.

During this time period, Hannah was tested and found to have some attentional issues and specific learning disability in the area of rote memory. Provided with the support she required, Hannah went on to be a successful student in school, finishing several honors courses in high school and earning college credit before the end of high school. She proved to be an amazing writer with creativity beyond her years, and she enriched her own high school experience by choosing to take Animal Science classes rather than typical electives.

As her mother and as a teacher who works in this way, Debbie has often thought about the gift she and Hannah were provided through Hannah having the opportunity to experience and grow in her strengths so that she "felt smart." But the additional gift of having such a clear record of Hannah's capacity for intelligent and masterful thought and representation gave her parents enough information to know that the inability to grasp those early academic skills did not define Hannah's abilities in any way and provided incentive to have the necessary assessments completed. There is no doubt in Hannah's or her parents' minds that she would have had a completely different experience in her school years without this valuable information.

SUMMARY

In order to provide young children with the opportunity to grow in their own strengths, engage in their own interests, and overcome challenges, adults working with those children must start their relationship with the willingness to learn more about the child at the very beginning of the year.

The commitment to observe young children requires that teachers let go of their traditional planning and allow for more flexible and child-centered preparations as the year begins. Planning around the routines of the day rather than creating teacher-directed activities that require a significant amount of adult supervision is a strategy for allowing additional time for observations. Allowing children the freedom to choose their own areas of interests along with the use of time-sampling charts allows teachers to observe children more fully. In doing so, teachers learn about the children's interests and the areas they tend to avoid, and the teachers also glean information about the children's temperaments, strengths, and challenges.

Observing children in their natural play and creative endeavors also allows for more authentic assessment of children. Extensive observation of children at the beginning of the school year and reflecting on those observations allows teachers to glean information about students early in the year. This, in turn, promotes greater understanding of children's strengths, interests, intentions, motivations, and behaviors.

Teachers can make time for observations through capitalizing on the talents of instructional assistants, limiting the number of children who begin the year by implementing a phase-in system, collaborating with therapists, accessing parents, and asking for volunteers.

Creating an environment that is conducive to observation by setting up the physical environment as a third teacher and using materials that are open-ended allow teachers more time to observe children's interests, strengths, temperament, social skills, levels of play, and learning styles.

Lesson plans can be developed around routines rather than around specific activities that require extensive adult supervision. Lesson plans should be flexible at the start of the year in order to allow children's interests and ideas to become a part of those plans.

Assessment of children as a result of such observations can be achieved by varying means. Utilizing checklists while observing children allows teachers to learn about concept and skill knowledge of the children as the children are in their natural state of play. The use of pictures during play provides a documentation of children's play, work, and ideas, and this aids the teacher in seeing the child through a different lens. Placing sticky notes or index cards throughout the room enables adults to record an observation easily. Small notebooks or clipboards placed in the different centers allow adults to write observations having to do with that particular center.

An effective method for organizing each child's work is to create a portfolio. Portfolios inform all adults who work with the child: the teachers, the instructional assistant, the therapists, and the family. Portfolios are, in essence, a compilation of a child's work, ideas, interests, strengths, imagination, knowledge, and skill and concept development. The inclusion of pictures provides significant information to those who are involved with the child. Conversations that children engage in among themselves and with teachers can be documented and included in the form of text or recordings. Children's actual work samples and art should be included, or pictures can be taken of such work so that the children are able to bring their work home to their families. Children's story ideas can be dictated to adults and included in the portfolio. In addition, checklists of skills, ongoing assessments (both informal and formal), and anecdotal records written by the various adults who work with the children should be a part of the portfolio.

Information gleaned from taking the time to observe children in the beginning of the year is invaluable in providing opportunities in which children become intentional learners. As gathered information is used to create learning opportunities for children according to their own interests, children become active participants who are invested in their own learning process.

CHAPTER 4

Developing Play and Social Skills Through Emotional Regulation

It is fundamental to a strengths-based and emergent curriculum to arrange the personnel, space, and necessary time to help each child meet her or his emotional needs. By creating an environment rich in materials and activities that speak to each child's strengths and by validating each child's feelings, every child becomes invested in the "work" and emotionally comfortable with the setting. This engagement and bond with the environment allow each child to develop steadfast emotional and social connections with the teachers and peers. This comfort and the connections then begin to set the stage for moving each child's development forward across all domains. This chapter will focus specifically on the significance in supporting each child's emotional regulation to promote social and play skill development.

There are many resources available to support educational teams in determining ways to manage children's behaviors that they deem to be too disruptive or intolerable. Dan Gartrell, author of *The Power of Guidance: Teaching Social-Emotional Skills in Early Childhood Classrooms* (2004), describes such disruptive or intolerable behaviors not as misbehaviors, but rather as mistaken behaviors. Mistaken behaviors remind all who work with young children that learning how to regulate and adjust to new environments and expectations is a learning process. Throughout this process, even in adulthood, we all make mistakes (Gartrell, 2004). The focus of this chapter and Chapter 5, and of the book in general, is to engage children in relationships, interactions, and guided explorations of materials and the environment. When the adults facilitate learning experiences for the children based upon their interests, the children are actively engaged. Actively engaged children are interacting, discovering, and learning.

SUPPORTING EMOTIONAL REGULATION

In Chapter 3, the vignette with Juanita introduced the idea of how essential it is for children to become emotionally connected to people and interests in their environment at the beginning of the school year. It is typically expected that some of the children will need the 1st week or 2, maybe even a month, to feel comfortable at school. Yet, as educators, we are keenly aware that some children are not emotionally regulated within a month.

There are those children whose behaviors clearly demonstrate that they feel emotionally dis-regulated. These children are challenged to actively participate in their school experience. Think about the child who is bossy to others, claiming all of the materials for him- or herself and possibly bullying others who wish to join in play. Would this child be ready to collaborate or co-construct with other children, learning from them, as they play? Can we expect a child like Juanita, who does not freely separate from family or comfortably handle transitions and connect with others in new situations, to benefit to her potential from her school experience?

Trent's Story

Trent and his mom came into his new preschool classroom for an open house visit along with five other children and their parents. As expected, it took a few minutes of clinging to their parents for many of the children to feel comfortable in the classroom, but the excitement of novel toys and activities quickly replaced their apprehension, and within a few minutes the children were playing happily among their new classmates. There was one exception: Trent continued to sit on his mother's lap, anxiously surveying the room and retreating further into his mother's arms when the teacher approached him. Knowing that children sometimes need more time to feel comfortable in a new setting, his teacher allowed him his space, yet sat nearby and chatted with his mother in order to make herself more familiar to Trent. The first day of school, Trent was extremely agitated and fearful, and unlike the majority of his peers, he shrank from any attempt the teachers made to comfort him. While a few of his peers had similar reactions to the separation process, there were two aspects of Trent's behaviors that alerted his teachers to a possible challenge for Trent: his extended period of anxiety in the classroom, and his lack of social reciprocation, especially in the form of eye contact.

His teacher's concern increased when, after a few days, Trent's fears did not seem to abate at all. Upon arrival he would escape to a corner of the room and turn his back to the class, crying and rocking himself for comfort, but not allowing the teachers to provide any comfort, either physically or verbally. Just coming too close to him would initiate a heightened demonstration of anxiety and fear. In addition, Trent resisted any attempt to make eye contact with him. It took over a month of his teachers using multiple strategies before Trent was able to come into the classroom without exhibiting fear and extreme anxiety.

Opinions are plentiful and mixed about young children whose emotion-driven behaviors do not comply with the routines of the school and who are deemed too disruptive. Some opinions include: "That child is not safe around other children." "That child is disrupting the whole class." "That child should be sent to the principal or home." For the young child who is disengaged with the activities in the class and chooses self-stimulatory behaviors that do not appear disruptive to others, there are some who feel that keeping the child safe and caring for his or her needs is a "good enough" goal.

As teachers, therapists, parents, and administrators, some of us may question whether spending time and resources to make sure that each child is emotionally connected to the environment is sound practice. It is common to hear arguments such as, "We don't have time to deal with their feelings." "We have to get these kids ready for kindergarten." "They have to know their numbers and letters now so that they can begin to read by kindergarten and first grade."

This manner of thinking reflects a view that early childhood education is actually preschool and that our primary responsibility to young children is to prepare them for the academics of their real school years. To the contrary, we know that during the early years, young children are developing the foundations for learning and living throughout their lives. Children who enter school-based programs demonstrating emotional and behavioral challenges without support to meet those challenges are likely to experience challenges throughout their school careers (Campbell, Shaw, & Gilliom, 2000; Koplow, 2007; Mitchell & Hauser-Cram, 2009; Winsler, Diaz, Atencio, McCarthy, & Chabay, 2000). The National Research Council Institute of Medicine (2000) stresses that "Programs that combine child-focused educational activities with explicit attention to parent–child interaction patterns and relationship building appear to have the greatest impacts," and that "Some of the strongest long-term impacts of successful interventions have been documented in the domains of social adjustment" (p. 11). We also know that living involves so much more than the academics we all have learned at school. Expressing and coping with our emotions, comfortably socializing, and developing, and hopefully maintaining, our zestful inquisitiveness are aspects that bring added richness to our lives.

Feeling More than Just Happy, Sad, or Mad

Most of us who spend our days with very young children do a fine job of singing songs, reading storybooks, and using puppets to introduce feelings and feeling words. We realize that children are developing their feeling vocabulary and that this type of vocabulary will help them to express their emotions to adults and to their friends. As early childhood teachers, we reinforce our teaching of the feeling vocabulary by reminding children to "Use your words." We run the danger of falling short, however, when we reduce children's feelings and the vocabulary that we teach to "happy," "sad," or "mad."

Young children experience strong feelings as they explore and encounter the world around them. "Happy," "sad," and "mad" only begin to describe the range of feelings that any young child might face as she or he encounters new experiences throughout the day. Imagine trying bungee jumping for the first time. As you free-fall, bounce, and land, could you possibly limit the description of your sensations to happy, sad, or mad?

Empathize for a moment with a young child encountering the sights, sounds, smells, tastes, textures, touches, movements, expectations, personalities, and temperaments of a new setting and the people in it. Compound these new experiences with the fact that many of the young children we work with are not able, cognitively, to realize that their intense sensations are feelings, that everyone experiences them, and that they are temporary. Add the potential that our young children only have the words "happy, sad, mad, or no" to describe what is happening to them. Worse yet, what if they have no spoken language to communicate how they are feeling? Now imagine that you are bungee jumping in a new place, without anyone you know for support, and without speaking the language of the strangers who are there. Would you still only be feeling happy, sad, or mad?

CREATING AN ENVIRONMENT OF EMOTIONAL CONNECTEDNESS

Self-regulation and the capacity to form and learn through relationships is a strength for young children. Some children begin to gain more independence by leaving their family members for a few hours a day and going off to an early childhood school. This strength permits the child to affirm that his or her family will return for them when school finishes and that the family has chosen this setting knowing that their child will be safe and well cared for. The child will use these new attachments to form relationships with and learn from others at school.

One way to support young children in feeling heard and respected and to facilitate their self-regulation skills at school is to teach to each child's emotional development. It is our responsibility to facilitate young children's learning of emotional regulation, just as we focus on teaching colors, numbers, and letters. As we work with young children, we enhance their emotional development more fully when we identify, distinguish, and name all of the feelings that the children are experiencing. As we all have witnessed, children feel frustrated, annoyed, scared, startled, surprised, excited, unsure, disgusted, and so on every day. Calmly naming all of these feelings for young children helps them to identify and therefore contain their feelings (Koplow, 2007; National Research Council Institute of Medicine, 2000; Siegel, 1999). This is especially necessary when children experience intensely strong feelings. For example, if a child is attempting a task and is consistently struggling with it, providing that child with the definition of that feeling as frustration provides a label for the child to relate to the emotion he or she is feeling. Unidentified frustration to a child may literally feel like her or his insides will explode. However, by calmly naming the sensation for the child, he or she realizes that this feeling exists, has existed for others, has a name, and that it only feels like his or her insides will explode. The feeling and the reaction to that feeling may still be intense for the child. However, by showing the children our capacity to handle the intense feelings and by identifying the name of the feeling, we have helped to cage the wild beast of a feeling inside of them.

As we guide children in play, we have opportunities to embed this learning by matter-of-factly identifying the feelings they are experiencing and naming them right as the children experience them (Koplow, 2007; National Research Council Institute of Medicine, 2000). Some examples of what this might sound like are: "Wow! I am hearing a lot of yelling voices. You all sound angry." "Oh boy! We saw a fire truck go by with its sirens on. That felt exciting." "That was a really loud noise. That was startling!"

Again, the teaching goal is to support our young children in realizing that they are experiencing the sensations of emotions, emotions have names, we all experience them, and we can gain support for our feelings when we identify them to others (Koplow, 2007). Some of the children in our midst will begin to label their feelings as they work and play. Others will not be able to label their feelings right away. However, all will begin to acquire from the adults the capacity to handle strong feelings. Also, including emotional regulation lessons for small or large groups with social stories written around their strong feelings, group discussions about feelings that we all experience, and ideas about what we should do with these strong feelings will normalize the feelings for each child. Often, the children with really intense feelings take the role as the expert in this area and demonstrate or lead the discussions. Yes! Even children who demonstrate intense, disruptive behaviors may use their experiences as a strength to teach peers about handling our strongest feelings!

Using Relationships to Promote Emotional Regulation

Trent and the many other children with whom we work who struggle to regulate their emotions teach us one thing: Children cannot begin to access their strengths to attend to, care about, or master other skills until they are emotionally regulated, comfortable, and invested in their learning environment. Young children rely on their primary caregivers, the parent, babysitter, or teacher who is with them throughout the day to serve as a home base from which they can bravely explore and learn from their surroundings. They also rely on these adults to provide guidance, redirection, and protection when their exploration becomes dangerous. We want children to curiously explore developmentally appropriate materials that have been set out for them on the rug, on a table at their height, or in a sandbox. Yet as we all know, when secure and consistent connections to caregivers and their developmentally appropriate expectations have not been established and enforced, young children's exploration of and adjustment to the world around them can be riddled with anxiety and caution or dangerously haphazard choice-making. It is our job as the adults to arrange the environment so that children cannot reach or use items in ways that will be dangerous to them at their young age. It is up to us to set these clear and consistent limits and make sure that the young children understand and follow them.

When the adults create caring, comforting, and consistent classrooms, young children feel respected and learn to relate to others in a respectful manner. Forming solid and secure attachments to others at school helps young children to regulate and flourish in the new setting. These connections provide the secure foundations from which children can separate from their primary caregivers, enter the new school environment, make their needs known, have their needs met, learn and follow new routines, engage in new and possibly challenging school experiences, and develop and enjoy these new relationships and experiences. The children can use their strengths to make emotional connections to materials and others in the school environment (Greenberg, Cicchetti, & Cummings, 1990; Koplow, 2007; Marvin, Cooper, Hoffman, & Powell, 2002; Meins, Fernyhough, Wainwright, Das Gupta, Fradley, & Tuckey, 2002; Winsler et al., 2000.)

Forming an Early Play Relationship

Although Trent was eventually able to come into the classroom with less anxiety, his teachers observed several characteristics that continued to concern them: his language was somewhat delayed for his age and was echolalic and repetitive rather than used in a meaningful way, he would move away from teachers or peers if he was approached, and his play was repetitive in that he would line up animals or cars but would not play in a symbolic or interactive manner. This concern led to a conference with Trent's parents. After a discussion of concerns that the parents and teachers felt about Trent's development, the decision was made to begin the referral process to their local school system to have Trent evaluated for developmental delays.

However, in giving the time to both help Trent regulate himself emotionally and observe him in the classroom, the teachers began to notice several of Trent's strengths and interests. He was very interested in playing with animals and dinosaurs and knew many of their names. He was very attentive during songs and books involving animals and would repeat the script of several animal books in the classroom.

Given Trent's interests in animals, his teachers decided to try to relate to him through that avenue. Debbie would approach him with a plastic animal, which he would move away from at first. She would follow at a distance and talk to Trent's animal with her own plastic animal. After some time he was comfortable enough to allow her to play alongside him. Gradually, she was able to create scenarios in which his animals and her animals connected within the play, creating playful obstructions with her animal as they played. For example, her lion might block his elephant, requiring him to go around her, push her lion out of the way, or ask her to move. His teacher's intent was to produce as many circumstances as possible in order to create as many circles of communication as possible as they played (Greenspan & Wieder, 1998).

Once she had established a level of comfort in their play, she began to extend the play to include peers in the classroom. Trent's teacher found that she had to stay in the play at the outset, in order to support each child in the interactive process (Hollingsworth, Able Boone, & Crais, 2009). However, after some time of establishing some modes of play, certain children would initiate play with Trent. While this was often a parallel level of play, it was exciting to see him play alongside peers.

Preparing the Classroom to Foster Emotional Connections

Surveying families about each child's interests and ways of calming prior to the beginning of our school year (Chapter 2) and observing and arranging provocations that speak to each child's interests (Chapter 3) helps us as teachers to arrange the classroom environment to meet and foster each child's emotional connectedness and development. Many of us create centers that include dress-up, dramatic play, writing, housekeeping, sensory, science or discovery, building materials and vehicles, books, or computers. That is, we create centers that will speak to each child's kinesthetic, musical, natural, logical-mathematical, linguistic, spatial, interpersonal, and/or intrapersonal intelligences and personal passions. Through becoming engaged at school, each child forms connections with others and begins to feel appreciated, cared for, and a member of the class community. Amy Casey writes in her article, "The STARE: The Scale for Teachers' Assessment of Routines Engagement," "When children are actively engaged with their environment, they interact with others more, manipulate materials more, and therefore learn more" (Casey & McWilliam, 2007 p. 3). For all of our children whose strong emotions drive their compromising behaviors, the process of becoming emotionally attached to others and calm while fostering their interests is particularly essential. Our challenge then is to work toward setting up the environment to meet each child's emotional needs and interests (DiCarlo & Vagianos, 2009; Harte, 2009; Hollingsworth et al., 2009; Koplow, 2007).

Michael's Story

Michael joined our class after the school year began. His adaptive, cognitive, and significant language and articulation challenges were compounded by his paralyzing unease when adults or other children could not understand what he was saying. Michael's parents were, and continue to be, vital partners in Michael's success at school. Before he entered the class, his parents thoroughly filled out the parent survey on Michael's interests, skills, and concerns. His teacher was able to set up the environment to help him form connections beginning on his very first day. A few dirt bikes and four-wheelers, in addition to the other vehicles in the building area, spoke to some of Michael's passions that his parents had identified. Despite his reservations with meeting and attempting to communicate with others, the dirt bikes and four-wheelers enticed him to play with them and with the other children who shared those interests. Michael was immediately accepted and sought after as a new friend who likes four-wheelers and dirt bikes too.

In addition to Michael's parents, the speech and language therapist brilliantly planned his therapy based upon his passions and his emotional needs. The teacher and therapist quickly observed that any time Michael was called upon to verbally answer a question he looked down and shook his head no or randomly answered "mud." (His passion for four-wheelers was equaled by his passion for the mud they ride through!) His therapist realized that if she drilled Michael on sounds that were difficult for him to produce, she would trigger his strong emotional response to shut down. Rather, she gave him ample time and opportunities to use his interests and passions to connect with others and activities in the environment.

She understood that if Michael could build up his emotional comfort with communicating and interacting with friends and teachers, he would be more receptive to addressing his articulation challenges. She was so right! Michael spent the year interacting and steadily increasing his conversations with friends around vehicles and then woodland animals, especially deer and turkeys. His growing emotional connectedness, comfort, and confidence eventually expanded his play into the housekeeping area, where he cooked and played family and pets with another set of friends. His interests also inspired him to further develop his fine motor skills in order to represent four-wheelers. All the while, his speech and language therapist joined the interactions, modeling strategies for introducing vocabulary words and phrases that the group could use to initiate, embellish, and sustain their play together (Hollingsworth et al., 2009; Jung, 2007).

Michael's Four-Wheelin' Bulletin Board. One day, Michael's teacher printed out multiple copies of pictures of four-wheelers and dirt bikes. She placed the pictures on a table with markers, collage materials, glue sticks, and scissors. Eager to work with the pictures, Michael began drawing, cutting, and gluing.

As friends joined Michael, the interest and conversation turned to wanting to make four-wheelers that actually had four wheels. (The printed pictures only showed two of the wheels.) Once the group had made paper four-wheelers (see Figure 4.1), Michael's teacher put him in charge of finding a place to hang all of the four-wheelers.

Michael and a friend chose to decorate a Four-Wheelin' bulletin board (see Figure 4.2). Michael's friend measured the board to determine how tall their mountain of mud could be. The friends worked together to place and staple all of the four-wheelers. Michael also requested help from a friend who was good at writing. He described his bulletin board and asked if she would write the sign for him. Michael told her what colors he wanted and she wrote the sign.

Facilitating Trent's Social and Play Skills with Peers. During Trent's first year, one specific book about animals was read that Trent would repeat on a daily basis. This book was read in the reading corner, a cozy and fairly close space in the classroom. The draw of the book created a second opportunity to help Trent become more comfortable in close proximity to peers and teachers.

Figure 4.1.
   Michael Cutting
   Copies of Four
   Wheelers

Figure 4.2.
   Michael and a
   friend Hanging
   Bulletin Board

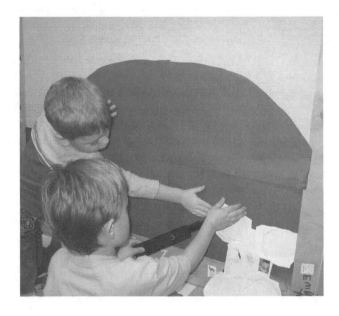

Eventually Trent was able to read the book to classmates, as he had memorized the text. Again, this provided more opportunities to connect and create circles of communication (Greenspan & Wieder, 1998).

The next year, Trent's play was focused on hearing stories being read, enjoying the dress-up materials, and creating patterns with any material to which he had access. Trent appeared comfortable returning to school, yet was not engaging with or joining other children in play. His play remained isolated. He slowly began to narrate his play to a teacher who happened to walk by, or to call the teacher's attention to a pattern he had created with blocks. Other children would take an interest in the dress-up clothes he was using or the patterns that he was creating, but Trent was not able to sustain the interaction.

One day as Trent lined up some large, colorful, wooden beads on the table, he mumbled "tomatoes and garden" to his teacher. The teacher sat down with Trent and asked him what was growing in his garden. Other children, interested in gardening or perhaps in the dramatic story line that Trent was creating, started to gather around the garden. He told us that the red, round bead was a tomato; that the orange, rectangular bead was a carrot; and that the yellow, round bead was a lemon. The conversation turned to all of the silly vegetables growing in the garden. Trent delighted himself and the other children with the odd and fanciful bounty in the garden. Together, they giggled and created bead vegetables in the garden.

Trent had made connections with other children in the room who shared his interest in both dramatic play and humor (Fitzgerald & Craig-Unkefer, 2008). His idea about the bead garden and about unusual vegetables not only captivated the interest of his peers, but sustained their interest throughout the interaction. From that day on, Trent became the "guy with fun, cool ideas." Later that year, Trent went to the studio within the classroom and found a domino. He also found a supply of circular yard-sale pricing stickers. Trent called the domino a "jinga box" and decided to decorate himself as a jinga box (see Figure 4.3.).

Excited with Trent's idea and his competence in choosing and representing with the materials, two of his friends decided to also make jinga box dominos. They chose to make their jinga box dominos out of boxes. In their article, "Individualized Inclusion Plans at Work in Early Childhood Classrooms," Hollingsworth et al. (2009) stress the use of evidence-based

Figure 4.3. Trent Decorating Himself as Jinga Box

interventions to promote social skills development for young children with disabilities. One recommendation is to use naturalistic strategies. Naturalistic strategies involve setting the play environment with innovative and open-ended materials that require the children to converse and negotiate about how to use the provocations (Hollingsworth et al., 2009). Just as Michael needed to communicate with his friends about the four-wheelin' bulletin board, Trent and his set of friends talked to each other about creating jinga boxes. Although Trent's friends were interested in making jinga boxes, they were clear that they wanted to make traditional box dominos decorated with dots. They asked Trent if that would be all right. Trent assured them that it would and told them where to find the dots. Trent modeled how to apply the dots for his friends. Again, Trent used his interests, visual-spatial intelligence, and humor to reciprocally connect with peers. He communicated and demonstrated his ideas. He took on a leadership role as he directed others in locating and using the materials.

For the next 2 years, Trent's media of choice for representing color and pattern were drawing and painting (see Figure 4.4); he was particularly interested in abstract art. Trent would enter his already bustling classroom and go directly to the drawing materials. As he completed each of his brilliantly colorful drawings he would announce their subject and display them throughout the room. While watching Trent draw and appreciating the quality of his creations, another classmate cooed, "I just love Trent's drawings!" Others began to say, "I'm going to make one of those!"

**Figure 4.4.
Trent's
Drawing**

By encouraging Trent's early, detectable intelligence in patterning and spatial relations, his teachers were able to promote his emerging strength and outstanding ability to represent through drawing. They used these strengths, as well as Trent's abilities in dramatic play, costuming, and storytelling to promote his social skills. By starting with his strengths and directing those strengths toward roles in which he would feel comfortable and confident with his peers, Trent enjoyed seeking and being sought by the other children (Mastrangelo, 2009).

SUMMARY

As Michael taught us, it is young children's emotional connection to others, activities, and materials in their environments that then serve as catalysts for skill development in the other domains that have been challenging. Especially at the beginning of the year, it is important to choose and arrange items and groupings of children that will promote connectedness, emotional investment, and engagement for each child. Materials, open-ended activities, and groupings of children all play essential roles in this development (Ganz & Flores, 2010; Greenberg et al., 1990; Harte, 2009; Hollingsworth et al., 2009; Lytle & Todd, 2009). As we observed with Michael, deliberately and specifically arranging materials that speak to each child's interests sets the climate that feels comfortable and inviting, but also will serve to spur interactions with others and eventually development in areas that have been challenging.

Use the insights gleaned from parents to create a welcoming environment before the children arrive. By setting out a few of the specific books, vehicles, dolls, puzzles, dress-up clothes, manipulatives, colors, textures, smells, pillows, weighted vests, dough and clay hammers, and so on that your parents have noted help to calm or engage their children, the environment will already provide a sense of familiarity. The children will arrive those first days or weeks with many emotions. They may feel excited and eager, unsure and terrified, or furious and indignant. The environment should have materials that speak to each child's interests, but also serve to calm strong emotions. As we can imagine, snuggly pillows, blankets, dolls, dollhouses, books about families and feelings, pictures of families in journals from home, sensory bins with soothing materials, comforting scents, and even trampolines and heavy materials can calm the vast array of emotions that walk (or are carried) through the door.

Regardless of the type of emotion, we know that emotional regulation is essential to free children to develop in other domains (Koplow, 2007). Mary Polce-Lynch, author of *Boy Talk*, shares with us that: "Some theorists argue that it isn't possible to have a thought without a coexisting emotion. Among many functions, this powerful teamwork results in emotions aiding (or interfering with) memory and other cognitive abilities that help us to regulate our emotions" (Polce-Lynch, 2002, p. 7).

Working with young children who have very intense feelings may seem to drain the attention, energy and resources from the other children who are regulated and ready to move their cognitive development forward. Often a teacher or assistant is alone in supporting the rest of the children while the other adult supports an individual child to regulate his or her emotions. It is necessary as teachers to reach a balance of serving all of the children while allowing ample time and consistent support to the child or children in regulating their strong feelings. This takes communication, slowing down the pace of the room, attempting multiple strategies, and rethinking those strategies that give little support. This process is the gift that the adults and children give to each other in early childhood education. When we are knowledgeable of and honor how essential emotional development is to all of the other areas of development for young children, we afford the time, personnel, and opportunities for children to experience and express their emotions (Koplow, 2007).

We adults often feel compelled to end a child's strong feelings quickly so that he or she may get back to the lesson at hand. We do not want the other children to be disturbed or to become upset. We do not want to disturb the rooms near ours. We do not want it to appear that we do not have control over the children and their emotion-driven behaviors. We also, and at times rightfully, use our intuitive teaching sense to realize that eventually it is time for children to develop and move through their strong feelings. Research stresses that we move in these areas with caution and listening ears.

Many children turn to the adults at school for comfort when separating from their primary caregivers at the beginning of the year. They also turn to us to create an atmosphere which will hear, honor, and respect their needs while promoting their interests and development. In her book *Creating Schools that Heal* (2002), Leslie Koplow stresses that symbols (such as four-wheelers and jinga boxes) "generated from strong teacher-child relationships and developmentally appropriate collective experience will be elastic, strong, effective, and truly creative because they are personal, meaningful, and learned from intimate contact with people and things, not rote" (Koplow, 2002, p. 53). This symbolic representation and the development of cognition through strengths-based learning will be focus of Chapter 5.

Promoting Development Through Strengths and Interests

Educators in the early childhood field are increasingly cognizant of the need to actively engage children in their work in order to create a learning environment in which the child is invested and participates in his own learning. Relating to and responding to children's interests as a vital aspect of planning in our practice provides children with the opportunity to become more engaged in meaningful experiences and results in children becoming more curious, interested, and excited about learning (Jones et al., 1994).

It is our challenge as teachers to explore how we will both determine and encourage the interests of the children we teach. As was pointed out in previous chapters, the most effective way to determine the specific interests of a child is to observe the child in play with limited teacher-directed activities. In order to provide children with the time and space to demonstrate their interests, the classroom schedule and environment are most beneficial to children when set up in a manner that allows children to make some decisions about their own activities within the day (Casey & McWilliam, 2007; Jolivette, Stichter, & McCormick, 2002). Carol Gestwicki (1999, p. 101) addresses this need: "Because developing a sense of initiative is an important task of the preschool year, children's active participation as decision makers is enhanced by an environment that encourages making choices and plans. Much of their time will be spent in active play of their choosing, rather than in teacher-directed lessons."

CREATING LEARNING ENVIRONMENTS FOR MULTIPLE INTELLIGENCES

Supporting children's strengths and interests also involves creating an environment that allows for those strengths and interests to be expressed by children and observed by teachers. The classroom environment can be designed to support multiple intelligences through offering centers and materials that provide the spark that interests and intrigues children with a range of intelligences. Gardner's (1993) multiple intelligences theory informs us that there are multiple ways for children to be intelligent and that using these intelligences to teach provides children with strategies and motivation to learn in all areas. Effective teachers use this understanding in multiple ways.

For example, a child who has a strong intelligence centered on the natural world might best learn the concept of categorization using materials such as shells or rocks, rather than materials that often come as part of a curriculum. Children who are kinesthetic learners process knowledge through their bodies and therefore require the opportunity to move around and touch objects in order to learn skills that others may learn while sitting at a table with peers. Children with a visual/spatial intelligence learn best by visualizing, daydreaming, working with colors, drawing, and building. Affording these children with open-ended materials in art to represent ideas and process information provide them the opportunity to further their understanding of concepts and skills. Creating a block area that is rich in different types of materials can create rich learning experiences about size, shape, balance, and design, to name just a few.

A common strategy used by teachers of children of all ages, but particularly teachers of young children, is the use of music to teach and ingrain ideas, concepts, and skills over the curriculum. How many times a day does a teacher of young children use songs to teach the days of the week, rhyme, number sense, or transitioning from one activity or time of day to another? These are just a few examples of how we instinctively seek different modes from which to present and experience new information. If children, in their early years, are provided with experiences that allow them to feel confident and efficient in their ability to learn and create, they will more readily seize new problem-solving opportunities and use those intelligences to aid them in their acquisition of knowledge. (See Appendix B for a chart of multiple intelligences).

BECOMING INVESTED LEARNERS

When children are interested in the activities within the classroom, they not only show greater initiative and become more invested in the activities, they also have the opportunity to begin to think in a more abstract manner, increasing their ability to problem-solve and engage in reasoning skills (National Research Council Institute of Medicine, 2000). In order to follow through with interest-based learning there are beliefs that we must come to understand and embrace. They include:

- The competency of young children (Sussna, 2000; Vakil et al., 2003).
- The value of exploration as a vital part of the curriculum.
- The validity of allowing the time and space needed to provide children the opportunity to demonstrate those competencies.

PRESCHOOL IS NOT MINI-SCHOOL

With new understandings of brain development and the importance of children's opportunities to explore (National Research Council Institute of Medicine, 2000), the field of early childhood development and education has moved away from viewing preschool as a type of mini-school. It is important that we are able to identify those differences in order to feel empowered to teach in the most appropriate manner for early childhood education. The idea of school brings up images of a classroom in which the majority of the children are engaged in similar activities, often seated at tables, with a teacher addressing the group and providing directions. While the concept of preschool naturally lends itself to allowing more time for play in centers and the teaching of more age-appropriate concepts, in the history of the development of preschool there have been cases of preschool looking too much like school. However, the understanding of how children learn has moved the early childhood field to an understanding that a much more active, exploratory teaching technique is, indeed, best practice (National Association for the Education of Young Children, 2009; Pretti-Frontczak & Bricker, 2004; Sandall et al., 2005).

However, there seems to be a lingering sense that in order to be taken seriously as teachers and to demonstrate that the children are learning, we, as teachers, are compelled to provide multiple activities that revolve around whatever theme or unit is being explored at that time. It is, in truth, one way to feel more secure that we are planning for learning. A busy classroom that requires children to complete one activity after another, however, does not allow time or a sense of calm to attend to children's individual interests and strengths (Sussna, 2000). In other words, lots of activities do not necessarily equal lots of learning. One more time—lots of activities does not equal lots of learning.

The question to ask when planning activities is: How actively engaged are the children who are participating in this activity (Casey & McWilliam, 2007)? When every child is seated at a table with the materials to make a duck, for example, and those children are required to make the duck by using shapes to make a body, beak, eyes, wings, and so on to create a particular and similar end product, there are certain skills or concepts that the teacher has most likely created in his plans as objectives for that activity. For example, the duck activity may include identifying colors, shapes, and positional concepts; using glue; exploring the texture of feathers; and following directions. But every teacher with experience knows that while a few of the children can complete that activity effortlessly and enjoy making that duck, those children are generally the very ones who already know most of those concepts. The children who need the most practice on those very concepts may likely be lost or distracted during much of this activity. They might need to have an assistant or teacher help them complete the project or they might choose to, pardon the pun, "duck" out of that activity through becoming distracted or exhibiting avoidance behaviors. This is not to say that there is never a place for this type of activity in a preschool classroom. However, if this is the type of activities that make up the basis of the child's learning in the classroom, it may appear that many of the children have just engaged in a learning experience when they were actually primarily just present during an activity. Again, preschool is not mini-school, it is a time to get children ready at the appropriate developmental level to be successful in school.

Using authentic experiences to address objectives, skills, and concepts individualizes learning and creates meaningful experiences that aid children in learning through the medium that best speaks to their learning styles. It is our suggestion that preschool is a time to not only learn those time-honored preschool skills such as colors, shapes, positional concepts, and so on, but more importantly, a time and a rare opportunity to learn something else that may never be afforded to children again in their educational experience. This learning permits children to:

- Find out what they are good at and are interested in
- Become curious learners (which translates into initiative)
- Learn that they have good ideas
- Learn how to plan, process, and follow through with plans
- Learn to follow through with activities (even when they don't want to) in order to achieve something they desire
- Learn how to negotiate with others in order to follow through with plans
- See that their opinion matters
- Be independent while still learning that others can help them further their ideas and plans
- Watch others in order to discover good ideas
- Help others further their ideas
- Go to peers and teachers to think and talk about ideas

When children are provided opportunities to learn based on their own interest and excitement, these concepts are learned as a part of the process. These concepts will provide children with tools that they will use not only in their early years, but throughout their educational career—and throughout their lives. In addition, if these ideas and concepts become a part of the child's own self-concept, then many of the personal-social goals of early childhood have been taught and learned through the process of experimentation and discovery that the child experiences on an ongoing basis and in a holistic manner (Booth, 1997).

An example of how an entire classroom can be enriched by following the interests of a child is the story of Evan and Fred. Evan commented during lunch one day that he had a pet ant, named Fred. He went on to tell Debbie and the children that Fred lived in his room and slept with him at night. In the past, that may well have been the end of that conversation for his teacher, chuckling to herself about his imagination. However, after using authentic experiences of children in her work for some years, she instantly recognized that this was something that Evan was very invested in. As the conversation about Fred continued, some of his peers listened and began to ask questions about Fred. That day they all learned that Fred had quite a life of his own. Fred went to ant school and played with ant friends while Evan was in school, coming back to Evan's room at night. Fred and his adventures created multiple learning opportunities during that school year. Evan wrote stories about Fred, the class as a whole noticed anthills on the playground, and Evan and his peers spent quite some time watching the ants with magnifying glasses to observe them carrying food. Noticing how the ant homes were rebuilt after a particularly strong storm one day, the children helped Miss Susan, quite a naturalist herself, set up an ant farm. Needless to say, that led quite naturally to interest in insects and bugs, which provided multiple opportunities to learn about insects while increasing skills and concepts, such as using insect counters to sort colors and types of bugs, read stories and recall, and so forth.

THE PLANNING PROCESS

How do teachers go about planning for the areas of cognitive, personal-social, and adaptive growth? These are, of course, areas that are primary in both typical early childhood development and in the areas of delay in children with developmental differences and delays. When children's interests and strengths drive the curriculum choices, planning is around the goals or objectives that the children are developing as they relate to the children's interests, rather than planning activities or themes and attempting to plug the goals into the theme. For instance, it is common for teachers to create themes for study that might develop from: the time of year (fall, winter, etc.), getting to know community helpers, an "All About Me" unit to develop self-concept, and so forth. Usually the ideas involved in creating these themes come from the teacher's ideas or from resources, such as an early childhood resource, or internet resources, or just talking with other teachers. In such a teacher-created theme-based unit on farms, the typical planning might involve creating centers, art projects, stories, and concept development activities for small- and large-group time, all of which would be centered around the theme of farms. The objectives and goals for children would be considered when creating those centers and activities, and the children would be expected to participate in the activities that the teacher has planned, therefore becoming exposed to the intended goals or objectives.

However, in creating teacher-directed lessons for all of the children in the class, there may be a risk that the objectives are not differentiated. The objectives may be teacher-directed or commercially directed based on the vocabulary and concepts of the theme. Farm objectives might be to use farm vocabulary; identify farm animals, tools, and crops; create farm animal puppets; and so forth. Even when we differentiate the level of theme-based objectives, such as having some children repeat the color of the animals or the sound of the animals while others sort farm crops by color, the objectives are still centered on the farm theme. Valid questions that we educators should ask are: Is it essential for each child that the focus of learning colors is on farm animals and crops? Do some of the children already know the colors of the farm animals and crops? If it is not essential that learning colors is centered around a farm theme, then let's consider color-name learning be embedded in naturally occurring, high-interest play and activities. The teachers' time and energy can shift from creating centers and activities in order to teach objectives around a theme, to authentically teaching each child's objectives so he or she may achieve his or her plans of interest.

For instance, if a child is particularly interested in farming vehicles and begins to talk about tractors in circle one day when the teacher has planned another activity, rather than just listening to the child's thoughts about tractors or perhaps stopping that line of conversation in order to get back to the activity at hand, a teacher who was seeking to engage children in the unit would take a short break from the current activity to listen to that interest and to make note of it in some form.

The understanding of children's interests is accomplished through the process of documentation and observation. This awareness leads the teacher to explore with the children what they want and developmentally need to know more about, or what may be speaking to their own learning style or intelligence. A result of this observation of the children is a willingness to become flexible with planning and allow children to use their own strengths and interests to provide input into where the unit of study will go while the teacher plans for embedding individualized learning objectives into routines, circles or small groups, schedules, and the environment, as well as materials and provocations provided. Children are encouraged to create their own version of what is needed in the classroom to complete their ideas.

Noting Children's Interests

The notation of children's interests may take the form of adding that idea to a list of possible projects on a whiteboard or pad of paper that stays in the circle area. This allows the child to understand that he or she has been heard and that the interest expressed is valid. Either during that circle, after the planned activity is finished, or at a later time in the day, the teacher can again address that interest with the child or a group of children and discuss ways to further that interest. Some possible ways to accomplish this might be to have the child go to the library to take out books on farm equipment (research), dictate a note to the librarian to help pull resources (early literacy), or make a plan to create a tractor, which furthers the adaptive development of initiation and engagement. The beauty of using children's interests in this way is that it not only engages and motivates the child, it also provides teachers with new ways of looking at units of study and with fresh, authentic learning opportunities.

As another means of creating authentic learning experiences, children can participate in the ongoing needs of the classroom, such as making signs for areas; creating calendar reminders of special events; and suggesting, voting on, and creating pictures to represent months of the year, which can then be used to create patterns on the calendar. (For example, in October children may decide to use pumpkins and leaves to create an A–B pattern for that month. Children are then recruited to draw those pictures to use in that way.)

Through the collaborative effort of adults working with children to express their interests and strengths, children are provided the ability to move beyond their own cognitive level of mastery into a higher level of thought, planning, and execution of ideas.

Planning to Support Children's Learning Through Their Interests

An essential tenet of the social learning theory by Vygotsky is that there is a zone of proximal development (ZPD) as children develop and learn. That is, there is a zone of cognitive development that the child cannot reach by him- or herself, but, given the support from an adult or a more capable peer, the child is able to develop those new skills or ideas. The sociocultural theory of cognitive development assumes that cognitive functioning grows out of social interactions during problem-solving and practical activity. This learning occurs in the zone of proximal development, which Vygotsky describes as the distance between the actual developmental level as described by independent problem-solving and the level of potential development as determined through problem-solving under adult guidance or in collaboration with more capable peers (Dodge et al., 2002). This guidance of others is referred to as scaffolding. Scaffolding is the process in which others adjust the level of help provided in response to the child's level of performance. After being provided that help, or scaffolding, the child moves from the zone of proximal development to independent skills and problem-solving at the new level of development (Vygotsky, 1978).

According to Vygotsky, it is through the context of the child's culture that he or she learns and develops cognitively. The culture of the child includes the culture of the family, school, peer groups, community groups, and so on, as well as the culture at large. It is through the culture of the child that he or she acquires much of the content of his or her thinking and problem-solving. The people who comprise the child's cultural environment, both adults and peers, provide the child with experiences that create opportunities for problem-solving, skill-building, and exchange of ideas, which lead to cognitive growth and development (Gredler & Shields, 2008).

Robert's Story: Scaffolding to Facilitate Personal-Social Skills and Representation. Robert was a child who had been diagnosed as being on the autism spectrum. Robert had many strengths: he had a sense of humor and a strong rote memory, and was very interested in math. Those strengths had been utilized to further his vocabulary and provide him with more activities related to the areas of letters and numbers in order to facilitate his ability to choose and stay with activities. However, Robert was not yet playing in a meaningful manner with other types of materials in the classroom. The teacher's attempts to engage him in block or dramatic play proved to be frustrating for all. Robert wanted to interact with peers but did not know how to do so.

Robert's teacher spent some time reflecting on this obviously bright child and how she might be able to move him further along the developmental ladder. Like many young children in the autism spectrum, Robert had a fascination with certain objects or activities. In Robert's case, one of those objects was ceiling fans. Robert had recently moved to a new home and had a baseball ceiling fan in his room. Robert talked about fans a lot. As his teacher reflected on Robert's obvious interest in fans, she began to consider ways to facilitate his development with the use of this strong interest.

To begin with, Robert's teacher took him to the block area and showed him how a cylinder block topped with two crisscrossed planks could make a representation of a fan. Wow! Robert found that to be amazing and made his own fan. Robert made many, many fans in the block area. His teacher watched and struggled with how many fans she should allow Robert to make before she pushed him to create something else in the block area, but decided to give him some time to learn about the affordances of blocks. She needn't have worried. As is often the case in an inclusive classroom, the other children in the room naturally became the teachers in the block area. As Robert spent time in that area he had the opportunity to watch other children create zoos, roadways, buildings, and other things, and he eventually began to experiment with block-building himself.

In order to take Robert's representation of the fan to a new level and to help him understand that he could begin to represent his ideas, his teacher provided him with wood, which was familiar because of his experiences in the block area, but moved him to the art area, so that he could create a fan sculpture that would be permanent. His motivation to move from the block area was twofold: He would still be building his fan with wood, and this time he could take this product home! (See Figure 5.1.)

Again, because of his opportunity to experience working with glue and wood, Robert became more interested in working in the art area. His teacher

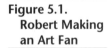

**Figure 5.1.
Robert Making
an Art Fan**

had been trying to move Robert into more meaningful play and realized a perfect opportunity! In the dollhouse there were, of course, bedrooms set up with bedroom furniture. Robert's teacher took him to the dollhouse and showed him the room for the little boy, and wondered if the little boy would like to have a baseball ceiling fan in his room. Robert thought that of course the little boy would want a ceiling fan! Robert's teacher provided him the materials to make a ceiling fan and talked to him about who lived in the boy's house, who visited the boy's house, what the boy did at his house, and so on as he made the fan.

Once the fan was complete and installed, Robert was motivated to play in the house. His teacher took on the role of the other people who lived and visited in his house, and she made suggestions about things they might do. With this adult support to move his thinking forward, Robert was able to begin to play in a more symbolic manner and began to make up his own scenarios about the boy (named Robert), based on his own true-life experiences. (See Figure 5.2.)

Just as before, the peers in his class were the teachers who took this play to another level altogether. As they began to join Robert in his play they thought up new and exciting adventures for the boy to go on, and Robert was able to begin to think about this boy in a more symbolic manner. At the same time, Robert was engaging in meaningful interactions with peers. With the scaffolding support of his teacher and his peers, Robert was able to move beyond his own level of development to a new level of representation of his ideas and interest and symbolic play.

Ricky's Story: Scaffolding to Facilitate Cognitive Development. An example of a child who moved forward significantly in his cognitive and adaptive development as a result of this collaborative process is a delightful child by the name of Ricky. Ricky had been in Early Intervention since he was 2½ years old and was diagnosed with general developmental delays. At 4 years old, Ricky, who would be entering kindergarten the next year, had very immature fine motor skills, using a fisted grasp with writing utensils. He was unable to rote count past three, had no concept of one-to-one correspondence, and was having difficulty with pre-literacy skills such as distinguishing same from different, answering questions related to comprehension, and identifying rhyming sounds. Ricky was not able to answer simple logic or wh- questions or employ problem-solving skills related to language. In group settings he was not willing to volunteer answers to questions, practically folding in on himself in order to avoid being called on.

Now, imagine this same child, by the end of the year, in charge of the planning, design, development, management, and construction of a workable, wooden play barn for the farm animals in his classroom.

With only 1 year to work with Ricky, Debbie was understandably concerned about the amount of work needed to provide him with as many tools as possible to take with him into kindergarten. However, she recognized the importance of taking the time to really observe Ricky to find out about his

Figure 5.2. Playing in the Dollhouse

strengths, passions, interests, and intelligences. Debbie immediately observed that socially, Ricky was a natural leader. His ready smile, his joy in new experiences and people, and his sense of humor won over all with whom he came in contact, including his teachers! Children sought him out and he was accepting of all children, regardless of their ability level. Ricky had a strong kinesthetic intelligence and loved the outdoors. The school system provided therapeutic horseback riding once a week to children receiving occupational therapy, and it quickly became apparent how enthralled Ricky was with this experience. Ricky was also very interested in building and creating new structures, and this interest aided other children as they began to build, watching Ricky as he problem-solved on this very concrete and physical level.

As Debbie continued to get to know Ricky, she strived to find a way to use his strengths to aid in the development of the areas in which he had challenges and, at the same time, help him to feel comfortable in taking risks in those areas, especially problem-solving in the area of language. She began to realize that Ricky seemed to be shutting down at circle time when questions of any sort were asked, as if he did not have the confidence to attempt any answers that might be incorrect. Debbie's goal for him was to feel comfortable about taking risks in order for him to practice his problem-solving and reasoning abilities. Her strategy in regard to this issue was twofold: she sought to provide him with questions that had no correct or incorrect answers and to allow him as much time as he needed to generate answers to those questions.

During this general time period, Debbie was also observing Ricky's strength in the area of construction and his ability to involve peers in that process. After observing him on several occasions, she came to understand certain aspects of Ricky's building skills. Ricky understood the basic techniques of building very well. He understood the need for a good base; could create a strong, tall structure; and had a very good eye for design for a child of his age. However, after really taking the time to observe over a period of time, she also noticed that the building only went so far. Once Ricky built the structure, he would generally just knock it down. It had not achieved a level of utilitarian use or representation of any of his ideas. On some days he and his peers seemed to use the blocks as a way to unleash some energy, just basically building to a certain point and then throwing them around until they were stopped by an adult in the room.

On one such day, Debbie stopped Ricky and his peers and challenged them to tell her what they were doing in the block area. "Building!" was, of course, the reply. "What are you building?" she asked. They looked at each other and then at the blocks. "We don't know," they replied. "Well," she said to them, "I'll tell you what: Why don't you guys take a few minutes and think about what you'd like to build for this area and then let me know? But I want you to stop playing with the blocks for a few minutes so you can really think about that." At that suggestion all three boys put down the blocks and began to move out of the area. (This was the beginning of the year and they weren't yet accustomed to being challenged in this manner.) Debbie quickly intervened, letting them know that leaving that center was not a choice. After this intervention (and a few moans) the boys, looking around at the center, spied the plastic cars. Ricky was the first to make the suggestion, "Let's make a garage!" Both of his peers were equally excited about the prospect. Debbie watched for a few minutes as they began to build. It became evident that all three boys had something different in mind, and those conflicting ideas were resulting in a hazardous building at best, creating frustration in all three children.

Debbie, having had experience with this type of scenario, took this opportunity to take their building and planning abilities to a new level. She stopped the boys and called them over to where she was sitting. "It seems to me that you guys need a plan to work from," she said. Debbie showed the boys some pictures of different types of architecture that were posted in the block area and explained that architects and engineers use plans when they want to build something. The boys were unclear about what to do, but Debbie assured them that she would help them through it.

This was a perfect opportunity to implement the concept of scaffolding. Debbie provided the boys with questions around which they could take their thinking further and visualize a plan for their garage. Some examples of questions asked of the boys included: What shape will your garage be? Do you want the garage to be one large building, or will it have many parts? Will your garage have a roof? What shape will the roof be?

Ricky and Lawrence created and used the plan they developed with the help of their teacher to make a big garage. The boys referred back to the plan as the teacher helped them to determine whether they were, indeed, building the garage in the way that they had planned.

The creation and follow-through of the plan provided opportunities for: planning, social negotiations, engagement, follow-through, early literacy, drawing lines (which is a prewriting skill), and answering and asking questions. The children also had the opportunity to reflect on their work in the form of comparing what they built as opposed to what they drew on their plans. During this process it was necessary to identify shapes, sizes, and numbers of blocks to complete the garage. But most important, it taught the value of planning, cooperation, and intentionality in their work.

As the children began to realize that with planning and the right materials they were able to create things they were excited about, several creations emerged in the room: puppet shows, books, dinosaurs, cars, and more. Toward the end of the year, Ricky began to talk about wanting to build a barn. After talking with him about his motivation for building a barn Debbie began to realize that he was actually envisioning a real, functional barn for his plastic horses at home. Of course! This was an extension of his passion for horseback riding coupled with the fact that he had realized that he was capable of making functional structures. Debbie agreed to provide him with the materials, assistance, and time for building a barn. His responsibility was to be the chief planner and architect in charge of the creation. While the whole class would have the opportunity to work on the barn, Ricky would be in charge of drawing and refining the plans, presenting color choices to the class, and deciding on final details.

In this way Debbie was able to present Ricky with the incentive to refine some of the skills he had been working on during the year such as answering wh- questions, improvement of fine motor skills, recognizing concepts such as same/different, counting, and using one-to-one correspondence in both the planning and building phases of construction of the barn. It also necessitated that he take a leadership role in large groups; he was, after all, the chief of this project. Ricky's classmates were enthusiastic about helping to build a barn. In order to begin the process of building a barn, Ricky was required to draw a plan for the children to follow in order to build the barn.

In Figure 5.3 Ricky is drawing the plan, which necessitated practicing the drawing of vertical and horizontal lines, a necessary step in prewriting skills. The children used scrap wood as the medium in building. Debbie allowed the children some time to process, sand, and build freely with the wood. Afterward, with Ricky as the mediator, they made some decisions about the exact shape and look of the barn through a voting process involving the whole class.

Placing the roof was difficult, as the short lengths of wood fell between the stalls. In Figure 5.4, the children used trial and error to problem-solve a solution: One center section of wood served as a base, which supported the remaining wood pieces. After gluing the wood pieces together, the children used hammer and nails to fortify the barn. Both the color and the name of the barn were decided through a voting process involving the entire class.

As the construction of the barn was coming to a close, Ricky was required to once again draw a representation of the barn into an architectural plan,

Figure 5.3. Drawing the Barn

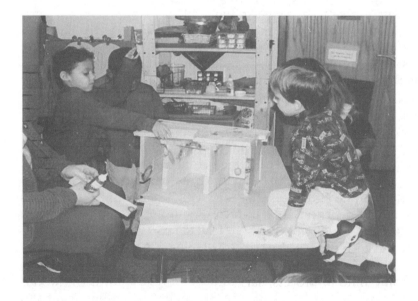

Figure 5.4. Building the Barn

with an emphasis on horizontal and vertical lines. Children in the class drew on the windows that Ricky had included in the plans.

As the school year ended, Ricky continued to be challenged in his skill levels and concepts. However, he made numerous gains in preparation for kindergarten: the confidence to speak up in a group, the ability to problem-solve using language, a much stronger understanding of concepts, improved fine motor skills, and, perhaps most important, the realization that despite the challenges he faced he also had many strengths and could create and represent his ideas according to his interests.

SUMMARY

Actively engaging children in their work creates a learning environment in which the child is invested and participates in his own learning. Learning about and planning around children's strengths and interests allows teachers to engage children in such a manner. Optimal learning environments and schedules are created with an awareness of the importance of allowing children to make some decisions about their own activities within the day. The classroom environment can be designed to support the multiple intelligences within each child, with centers and materials offered that provide the spark that interests and intrigues children according to their own intelligence.

When children are provided choices and encouraged to offer their own input and ideas about activities within the classroom, they not only show greater initiative and become more invested in the activities, they are also provided the opportunity to begin to think in a more abstract manner, increasing their ability to problem-solve and engage in reasoning skills.

A shift in thinking about early childhood education is necessary to provide children with authentic experiences that will encourage their own sense of exploration and curiosity about the world and a desire to learn. This shift moves away from thinking about early childhood development as a type of mini-school and toward a philosophy of allowing children to explore their own ideas, with teachers facilitating such exploration in the form of support and planning for new experiences and materials to be made available.

Using such authentic experiences to address objectives, skills, and concepts individualizes that learning and creates meaningful experiences that aid children in learning through the medium that best speaks to their learning styles. Working with young children in this manner allows for emergent and collaborative planning in which the children are a vital part of the process while providing children with tools that they will use not only in their early years but throughout their educational careers—and throughout their lives.

When children's interests and strengths lead the curriculum choices, planning is around the goals or objectives that the children are developing as they relate to the children's interests. The understanding of children's interests is accomplished through the process of documentation and observation. This awareness leads the teacher to explore with the children what they want and developmentally need to know more about, or what may be speaking to their own learning style or intelligence. While children are providing input into where the unit of study will go, the teacher plans for embedding individualized learning objectives into routines, circle time or small groups, the schedule of the day, and the environment, as well as materials and provocations provided in the classroom environment.

Vygotsky's social learning theory states that cognitive functioning grows out of social interactions during problem-solving and practical activity. Such learning is facilitated by peers and adults in the child's environment, using scaffolding strategies to provide children with the support to reach the next level of development, referred to as the zone of proximal development. It is through the choices that children make in play and during activities that they are able to make these important connections. Allowing children the freedom to explore choices that we may see as unusual or even, at times, perseverative in nature may be, in fact, allowing them the time to process their own ideas and make new connections, as was the case with Robert and his fascination with ceiling fans.

The use of children's interests to further concept development and skill levels is evidenced by Ricky's story. Ricky's interest in building and love of horses provided him with an incentive to move beyond his hesitancies and take risks in multiple areas of his learning, which led to advancement in his concept development, social skills, and skill levels, such as using fine motor tools.

Reflecting on both Robert and Ricky's experiences confirms Vygotsky's theory that children learn through their social environment and are able to take their development and skills to a new height when provided the scaffolding of others in the environment. When teachers reflect on children's interests and plan in a manner that takes those interests into consideration, and provide the support needed to take those interests further, children can go far beyond the typical expectation of their abilities.

CHAPTER 6

Planning Within a Strengths-Based Emergent Curriculum

Up to this point in the strengths-based process, children, families, educators, and therapists collaborate to discover each child's strengths—that is, their interests, intelligences, learning styles, and skills. These same members on each child's educational team build relationships and create the environment to support emotional and cognitive connections based upon those strengths. Now it is time to pull from best practices to develop learning opportunities that respect each child as a competent learner; promote skill development across all domains; and offer embedded opportunities for engagement, creativity, and higher-level thinking.

Paley (1986) observed that when devising these child-focused practices,

> the key is curiosity, and it is curiosity, not answers, that we model. As we seek to know more about a child, we demonstrate the acts of observing, listening, questioning, and wondering. When we are curious about a child's words and our responses to those words, the child feels respected. The child *is* respected: "What are these ideas I have that are so interesting to the teacher? I must be somebody with good ideas." (p. 127)

The emergent curriculum, negotiated between the children and the adults, grants us these best learning practices.

CHILDREN'S INTERESTS AS BEST PRACTICE

The evidence-based research cited in the Council for Exceptional Children's Division of Early Childhood's Recommended Practices substantiates child-focused practices and learning environments. Its authors emphasize creating adaptive and accessible play environments that "promote engagement, play, interaction, and learning by attending to children's preferences and interests" (Sandall et al., 2005, p. 77). By permitting children to negotiate the curriculum with the adults and with each other, we promote their growth and development even further. Not only do the children generate and communicate their good ideas, they also listen to others' ideas, compare and contrast ideas, communicate why they prefer certain ideas, compromise, practice being flexible and handling disappointments, delay gratifying all of their wishes, broaden their thinking and thought processes, gain the opportunity to regard the feelings of others, and much more (Angell, Stoner, & Fulk, 2010; Harte, 2009; Winsler et al., 2000). When driven and engaged in our own interests, the potential for learning life skills feels endless.

HOW A PROJECT EMERGES

Spring is the time of year that all preschool teachers recognize as the time of transitions for children who turn 5 during the school year and are excited about the prospect of being "big kids" in kindergarten. Those are the days when children tend to get loud, silly, and experiment with their newfound big kid status.

One spring, while observing children playing outside, Denise noticed that a group of children repeatedly explored how quickly toys with wheels, and even those without, can accelerate on an incline to achieve "awesome" liftoff. Within the school environment, some of these soon-to-be-kindergartners had been proclaiming that preschool is for babies, and that they were not going to play like babies. They wanted to experiment with how much air they could achieve during their liftoffs outside, not sing baby songs or play with baby toys, such as dress-up clothes. After giving a long, hard look and listen to what was captivating these kids, Denise decided to bring these children's liftoff interest into the class. On another day Denise set up ramps, springs, tubes, and balls for a small group. She invited this select group of children, who were continuing to struggle with the skill of connecting with peers, to have a turn with the materials as a group. Denise documented their initial protests, which included threats that they would just lie on the rug because they "don't want to play," and that they preferred to play "alone." She also documented what happened next with this group of 5-year-olds.

Savannah obligingly rolled a ball down the cardboard incline and then exclaimed, "Denise, look!" Aidan, who had been watching Savannah, exclaimed, "I have an idea! I have an experiment! If we have a strong enough ball, it can go down to the dungeon!" Denise asked, "Would you like to create a dungeon with these materials?" Sabrina, who had been quietly using the materials, interrupted with an eager, "No! They are a carnival!"

And that was it! At that moment Denise could hear, see, and sense that their great idea of using the properties of physics to make a carnival instantly captivated and motivated each of the children in this small group to engage and interact with purpose. The making of a carnival had emerged from the children as their next learning venue.

Planning the Emergent Carnival Project

As some of the children began to excitedly tell their ideas for carnival games, Denise handed the children clipboards and pencils so they could draw their plans (see Figure 6.1). Each child drew what his or her game would look like and explained how it would work. Denise recorded their dictation at the

Figure 6.1. Aidan's Plan for Carnival Game

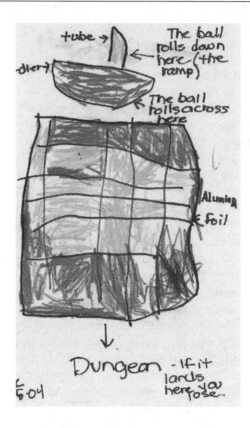

side of each plan. Their plans captured each child's initial enthusiastic and magical reactions to the notion of a carnival. They also served as catalysts for Denise's planning as one member of the carnival team. As she would do with any emerging project, a part of Denise's next tasks would be to:

- share the intentions with co-teachers
- observe whether the children continued to be motivated by this intention beyond that first meeting
- plan with co-teachers to meet with this group again to reexamine the plans and to begin a rich learning process of creating carnival games
- decide what learning could and should unfold along the process of planning, creating, and holding a carnival

For longer-range planning, Denise would need to begin to think about convenient and inexpensive ways to acquire the materials for the games. She would have to look at the class and school intentions and calendars to determine if it would be possible to commit time and staff to creating a carnival.

She would have to share the intentions and plans at the next staff meeting. Would the other staff members be interested in offering the space and resources for putting on a carnival? Who would run the carnival? Who would attend the carnival? Would the carnival planners need cotton candy machines and prizes? The planning for an emerging carnival project had begun.

A striking difference between planning for an emergent curriculum and planning for a teacher-directed curriculum is that the children are an integral part of the planning. Of course, the educators guide the decision-making and the time frames. Yet the children experience the excitement, creative flow, and empowerment of being the planners.

Enhancing Thinking, Communication, and Representation of Great Ideas

When Denise and carnival group members were able to meet again 5 days later, they looked and listened while each child shared her or his plans. Denise had wondered if the children would still be interested and motivated by the idea, but most of the children seemed just as enthused as they were 5 days earlier! The group brainstormed types of materials that they might use to actually make the carnival games. This process of generating ideas for materials gave the group an opportunity to think through how each game would work. While listening to the list of materials, the children began to envision how each game could work. They began to ask, "But if you use . . . how will it . . . ?" Or to comment, "I don't think it will fit!" The children continued with these collaborative and co-constructive dialogues until each child felt satisfied that they could make their game work. Denise recorded their proposed final lists of materials.

At their next meeting as a carnival group, the children tested whether their plans worked with the materials that were already available at the school. Some of those materials worked just as expected. They also realized that they had to gather other materials. The need for additional materials and help with carpentry spurred the children to share their drawn plans with their families. Denise reached out further into the community by inquiring at various shops if they carried the types of materials that the carnival group needed. She showed and explained their plans to employees in hardware and automotive shops. They suggested materials and other places to find specifically what the group needed. Denise also visited a local construction site where she was given what was left of an entire roll of Tyvek to make the monster maze. The carnival group also referred to the other children in the school, who were known experts, for making these other items for the carnival games. Here, again, is where documentation that is readily displayed informs all in the school of the interests and skills of each child. When the children in the carnival games group discussed all the pieces that they needed help making, the children and the teachers were able to name exactly who could help to get the job done!

Kamille wanted to create a "butterfly ride for your fingers." Anna was an expert on representing butterflies. She had been drawing, painting, and sewing butterflies in her classroom. She and Kamille took the plan for the

Figure 6.2. Girls Making Pipe Cleaner Butterfly Ride for Carnival

Up and Down Butterflies Ride to another child, who had been making but-terflies out of pipe cleaners (see Figure 6. 2).

The co-teachers planned opportunities for each child to use supplies to construct their game. They recruited other children who had strengths and/or interest in the construction process. Children with good listening and visual-spatial skills helped to test the game materials for size, angle, and fit. Those with strengths and plenty of practice in affixing and securing materials recommended the best types of adhesives and strategies for taping, gluing, and stapling into tight spots.

Once they had completed the plans for constructing the games, they were ready to plan the actual day. They called upon the children in each room who enjoyed using their artistic intelligences to decorate posters to advertise the Have-A-Ball Carnival. Children with linguistic intelligences who could write letters volunteered to write the name, date, and place on each poster. Everyone interested in making prizes for the games met in the studio to create prizes that "children would love to win!"

The youngest children in the school had been exploring music and move-ment. Some of the children in the class with the carnival project group had formed a rock band, playing the instruments that they had made earlier in the year. The adults booked a gig with both groups to play at the carnival so others could dance to the music. Denise asked another class to help prepare the snacks that parents had donated for the carnival. A different classroom of children offered to make ice cream for the carnival.

When the big day arrived, the whole school community came together to make the children's magical ideas of having a carnival come to life. The children ran their games, gave out the prizes that they had made, prepared and handed out snacks, and provided music and dancing. The staff provided support to the children running the carnival and opened other rooms and areas of the school for children who were not interested or comfortable with attending the carnival.

As evidenced by this story, allowing the children and teachers to follow their interests led to the richness of their learning. In her thank-you letter to the class for the Have-A-Ball Carnival, the director of the school, Irene Carney, applauded the children for their "great ideas and the hard work of making your ideas come to life." This is the essence of an emergent curriculum. It promotes supporting young children in thinking about "great ideas" and in confidently knowing that when they share those ideas with their peers and adults, children will be respected and honored with validation, opportunities, and resources.

Documentation in an Emergent Curriculum

It is important to emphasize again how vital documentation is to every aspect of learning through a child-negotiated and emergent curriculum. It is through observing and recording each child's interests that educators and the children discover their intelligences, how they best process information, what interests to pursue, and what areas of development pose challenges. The carnival began as a documented observation. A small group of children were engaged in experimentation when they were outdoors, yet refused to experiment within the preschool classroom. It was this documented observation that led to the carnival concept, the grouping of children by interest and skills, and eventually, the carnival.

During the carnival, the documentation evolved as the plans, photographic records, lists of things to do, agendas, announcements, and thank-you notes were created. The purposes of documenting every step of the carnival process varied. Certainly the initial plans that the children drew and from which Denise recorded their dictations served to record their intentions so that the group could move forward with them at the next carnival meeting. The group referred to those plans and their transcribed notes when they met to hear about each other's games and to begin to generate lists of needed materials. That documentation spurred both the children's memories of their intended plan as well as Denise's memory! The photos of the children testing the materials also documented their intention to use the materials. Likewise, the lists and agendas reminded the group of what they needed to gather and do and of places where Denise and families might try to acquire materials. By referring to and revisiting the various forms of documentation, the group remembered their intentions and expanded their thinking with hindsight.

A second role that the documentation played throughout the process of creating the carnival was that of providing inspiration. Being able to visualize plans, photos, prototypes of games, posters, prizes, and other children engaged in groups inspired children to join groups and to generate their own great ideas. As mentioned, anyone interested in joining a group or creating for the carnival negotiated with and communicated their intent to their peers and the adults regarding when, where, and how she or he might participate. During the second meeting of the carnival group, while eavesdropping on the explanations of the plans for each game, Kamille announced that she wanted to join and that she would create an up-and-down butterfly ride for fingers. Her great idea later inspired two other children, who both felt challenged by joining groups, to share their expertise in making butterflies.

Another child was so inspired by their great ideas and work that she decided to join too! (See Figure 6.2.)

Not only were the children inspired, but the documentation of their great ideas also motivated the staff to give over the space, time, and resources to having a carnival. The staff discussion of the project included:

- the desire to keep it based upon the children's great ideas
- the need to keep it manageable and therefore open the carnival to all the children in the school
- the realization that not every child in the school will be interested in attending the carnival, thereby creating the need for other rooms and materials to be open throughout the carnival week
- the need to flexibly accommodate the demands of the carnival: open teacher schedules to provide opportunities to create materials, prepare food, and rehearse music and movements; afford spaces to support the creation and running of the carnival; and to create opportunities for children to meet learning and physical challenge needs in alternate spaces

The documentation of the carnival also promoted reflection. The thank-you notes in particular offered opportunities for the children to thank everyone who helped bring their great ideas to life, such as their parents and the staff. The photos of the actual carnival provided all who participated and attended with the opportunity to revisit the work and enjoyment that went into running and attending the carnival. The thank-you notes to the children who ran the carnival afforded them the opportunity to reflect upon how hard it was to engage and interact to create and run the carnival. The notes also documented how successful the children were in using their strengths and interests to meet their challenges.

DETERMINING WHICH INTERESTS TO PURSUE

When we consider using an emergent curriculum, one question we ask ourselves is: If the children generate the ideas for an emergent curriculum based upon their own interests, what roles do we educators play in selecting and planning the curriculum and in embedding the developmentally appropriate goals and objectives? In an emergent curriculum, the adults facilitate the decision-making process of choosing which interest to pursue by monitoring the safety, soundness, and viability of the interests. To determine which interests to pursue, the adults ask themselves and others on the educational team such questions as:

- Is this interest safe and acceptable for young children to explore? How can we ensure safety and hear from our families and therapists that they are comfortable with the nature of the interest? Can we

modify the interest to make it more manageable and safe, and considered to be socially acceptable?
- How will the interest provide sound venues for learning and development? What will we do as a team to enhance the potential learning related to the interest?
- How viable is this interest? Consider the:
  » Number of children sharing this interest
  » Resources available (including the availability of adults to guide the interest)
  » Time and other constraints
  » Need to plan for a large or small group
  » Need to acquire or create materials
  » Need to create a meeting and working space for the children
  » Interest and its potential to drive the learning
  » Keeping the developmental goals and objectives of each child in mind, which goals and objectives will the children work toward through their interests and plans for pursuing this interest?
  » What system will we use to record data on the children's work toward mastering their goals and objectives while they follow this interest?

The National Association for the Education of Young Children's (NAEYC) position statement on Developmentally Appropriate Practice in Early Childhood Programs emphasizes that when young children are encouraged to be "active constructors of their own understanding, who benefit from initiating and regulating their own learning activities and interacting with peers," the adults must "strive to achieve an optimal balance between children's self-initiated learning and adult guidance and support" (National Association for the Education of Young Children, 2009, p. 17).

PROVIDING PROVOCATIONS WITHIN AN EMERGENT CURRICULUM

Provocations are the specific materials that we teachers arrange for a center, a small group, or the whole class that serve to promote experimentation and discovery in our young children (DiCarlo & Vagianos, 2009; Harte, 2009). They also serve as catalysts for in-depth exploration and research by the children. The children in the vignette certainly were fascinated with testing accelerating speeds and liftoff outside, but had not begun to make such associations with materials in the room. In fact, when the intended children first noticed the inclined blocks, materials that would roll, and clear tubes in a center, they glanced, at most, at the materials, and walked right by them. Instead, a group of children who were enjoying dramatic play began to add the materials to the cars they were building with the class chairs.

This observation informed Denise that she had to quickly plan with her co-teachers to create a small group around the specific children and these chosen materials. After other children in the class began to create their own intentions with the pieces of materials (see Figure 6.3), such as using the tube as an exhaust pipe for their car and the inclined block as a ramp to their bus, Denise announced that she would be inviting children to come and use the materials in the area by the wall of mirrors. The use of the word "inviting" brings the connotation that it is a special treat to use the materials, but also lets children, again, have a choice to decline the invitation. By providing provocations such as inclined blocks, materials with wheels and that roll, and clear tubes from inside the classroom, this select group of children had the potential to expand their thinking about acceleration and liftoff. They began to realize that they also could use the acceleration achieved on inclines to propel balls in a carnival game!

THEME-BASED CURRICULUM VERSUS THE EMERGENT CURRICULUM

Let's now compare the benefits of using a child-negotiated, emergent curriculum with those of teacher-directed, theme-based curricula currently used in most of our early childhood educational settings. Theme-based curricula usually follow holiday, seasonal, or other topics that the program creators deem educational and are often engaging to young children. Often these theme-based programs come prepackaged and are comprehensive. They may include plans, reproducible sheets, and props for activities. They address all domains of development and specify the age-appropriateness of the contents.

Figure 6.3. Aidan and Friend Looking Through a Tube

Figure 6.4. Girls Gathered to Play Fancy Egg Game

Administrators may consider it a benefit that these programs help to provide consistency to the content that their educators, across a program, will cover.

However, and this is a big however, the uniformity of theme-based curricula comes at the cost of respecting and honoring the ideas, decision-making, communicating with intent, compromising, and negotiating skills of young children (Koplow, 2007; Sussna, 2000). Also, we risk diminishing the effectiveness of our transdisciplinary approach when we follow holiday themes. A theme is a theme, be it Halloween Pumpkins or Carnivals. It is not the memorization of the facts of the theme, say, that pumpkins are orange or that jack-o-lantern is another vocabulary word for pumpkin, which is vital for the development of young children. In fact, the children in our vignette already knew the main concepts of a carnival: colors, carnival games, and prizes. Rather it is the wonderment, the experiences, the interactions, the realizations, and the processes that are essential for young learners. Through a child-negotiated and emergent curriculum, children have opportunities to wonder, theorize, explore, experiment, communicate, interact, share information and experiences, develop skills, attend to and learn from others, test, and question (Angell et al., 2010; DiCarlo & Vagianos, 2009; Ganz & Flores, 2010; Harte, 2009; Koenig, Bleiweiss, Brennan, Cohen, & Siegel, 2009).

As a result, it was the creation of and workings of the games that interested our carnival group. Sabrina was very explicit with her dad that the children playing her Fancy Egg Game had to be able to "see how it works" (see Figure 6.4). Thankfully, her father listened to and respected her intent when he assembled the game with her. The Council for Exceptional Children recommends that caregivers, educators, and therapists "facilitate children's engagement with their environment to encourage child-initiated learning that is not dependent on the adult's presence" (Sandall et al., 2005, p. 82).

In a child-negotiated and emergent curriculum, the learning, goals, and objectives are linked to the children's routines and play and, therefore, cross the environments in which they live, play, and attend school. Sandall and colleagues state that the aim is to "teach/promote the skills necessary for children to function more completely, competently, adaptively, and independently in the child's natural environment." Sandall and her colleagues further note that important skills for young children to learn in their development include:

- Being actively engaged with materials, objects, activities, and other people (peers and adults)
- Being an initiator (i.e., the child initiates play, social interactions, communicative exchanges, etc. without assistance from adults)
- Being responsive to initiations and behavior of others, including peers and adults
- Reading the cues of the environment and responding appropriately based on those cues without being directed by adults
- Having social interactions and relationships with family, peers, and others
- Communicating with others, including peers and adults (Sandall et al., 2005, p. 85)

We offer that these recommended skills and the developmentally appropriate goals and objectives for young children are effectively and functionally met through an emergent curriculum, negotiated amongst the children, their peers, and the adults in all settings (DiCarlo & Vagianos, 2009; Harte, 2009; Hollingsworth et al., 2009).

Facilitating Learning Through Interests

So how does following the children's interests "teach/promote the skills necessary for children to function more completely, competently, adaptively, and independently in the child's natural environment" (Sandall et al., 2005, p. 85)? As we saw throughout the carnival, the processes of planning for, requesting assistance for, creating, and holding their carnival offered multiple self-motivating, routine-based opportunities for learning. For the children who were trying to adjust to the idea that they were going to transition from preschool to kindergarten and do real work at a real school, the carnival employed the use and development of their cognitive and fine motor skills. For the children who had little interest in interacting with others, their desires to make a carnival necessitated and then fostered pleasure in working with others. Since the children initiated the concept of the carnival, each child became:

- actively engaged with the materials, their peers, and the adults
- a communicator with their peers and the adults at school and with their families at home

- responsive to their partners also working on the project
- interactive with their peers and the adults at school and with their families at home

As with any other interest, which we may have followed by putting out materials, choosing related storybooks, or inviting these select children to join a group working on a project, the topic may or may not have motivated them to overcome their challenges. However, by deliberately choosing provocations that spoke to their observed interests, these children were more motivated to become a part of the group in order to have the possibility of working with the materials.

Since the intent had emerged from the children, they felt empowered and responsible for their thinking, decision-making, and skill development (Koenig et al., 2009). They decided that they wanted to create a carnival. They determined whether they could master the skills and create every aspect of the carnival or if they needed to request assistance from and work with others. The thinking, decision-making, and skill development across domains and settings that took place throughout the process of making a carnival came with persistence, hard work, and much intrinsic motivation. The children took ownership for developing the skills necessary to create and carry out a carnival. They also took pride in their accomplishments, and rightfully so!

Bringing Together Theme-Based and Emergent Curricula

While considering an emergent curriculum we might also ask if it is possible to borrow from prepared, theme-based curricula to enhance our emergent curriculum. In her transdisciplinary, play-based curriculum *Read, Play and Learn!* Toni Linder encourages educators to follow the sequence of storybook activities that she has outlined or to follow "the interests of your learners" (Linder, 1999, p. 8). Even authors of theme-based curricula, such as Toni Linder, understand the importance of resourcing curricula according to the children's interests, strengths, and needs. We have found that these curricular kits can be useful sources of props, interactive materials, and activities. In addition, the teaching plans and tools that these authors present often serve as great starting points for educators because they offer examples of activities that may draw out great ideas from children. As one colleague put it, "There is no sense in reinventing the wheel" when these kits come complete with just the types of songs, stories, or games that may speak to the interests of the children in our classes.

So how do we use the materials and maybe even some of the activities from a kit and still reap the benefits of a child-negotiated and emergent curriculum? Or perhaps the real question is: How do we foster a child-negotiated and emergent curriculum while taking advantage of the compilation of materials from a kit? Let's look at an example of a literacy-based, theme-based curriculum involving the story "The Three Little Pigs."

If a teacher were to start designing a "Three Little Pigs" unit with the premise that each center should be set up in a certain way with specific, theme-based materials without considering the specific interests of the children, he or she might have a plethora of activities available in the classroom in which children are not particularly invested. If, on the other hand, the teacher were to note the children's interests as the book was read, the teacher may find that some of the skills that are to be addressed in the centers could be addressed in a more meaningful manner by speaking to the interests of those children.

A curriculum based on "The Three Little Pigs" may describe a creation of centers such as:

- Size differentiation of blocks in block area
- Dried straw or corn in a sensory bin
- Costumes in the dramatic play area
- Flannel board figures in the literacy center
- Retelling of the story with the children at circle time
- Using the opportunity to demonstrate how pink is made with red and white paint
- Cutting out paper to create bricks and straw to be used to create a picture
- Creating pig faces as masks in the art area

Our inclination as teachers may be to try to prepare the room before the book is read, arranging each center accordingly, fueling our own creative energies by pulling out and setting up materials for such activities. And many of the potential ideas for centers that we just listed are great ways to emphasize certain concepts and skills. Yet, in setting the centers up without gauging children's interests, we are presupposing that our efforts will speak to the interests of the children.

What if, when reading "The Three Little Pigs," the children actually became very excited about the idea of "blowing down a house"? Has this concept been reflected in the preplanned centers and small-group activities? What if the children were so fascinated with that idea that they begin to blow on one another to see their hair blow? Or what if, after circle time, the children began to pick up the paper or materials intended to be used in the art area for making pigs and instead start blowing on them? What would typically happen in a situation such as this? More than likely, the children will be asked to stop blowing the materials everywhere and leave their friends' hair alone. Some teachers may see the interest in the blowing and then have to choose whether to put on hold or even eliminate some of the centers already created and go with the interest in blowing, or to have the children continue in the prepared environment, because, of course, a lot of time has been invested in the preparations.

Now let's look at that scenario as a child-negotiated and emergent curriculum. Having decided to read the story "The Three Little Pigs," and after looking at the suggestions given in teacher-directed curriculum, what if the teacher decided to set up a few of the suggestions for centers, keeping in mind the preferences of the students in his or her class? The teacher may set up the block area with blocks of different sizes and weights, put straw in the sensory bin, and arrange the flannel board figures as a provocation for children, based on the interests the children have previously demonstrated. These activities do not demand extensive preparation, therefore allowing the teacher to change direction as needed and to follow the children's interests without a loss of valuable time and effort. In this scenario, as children decide to move forward with the blowing experiment, the teacher may have materials in mind or ready to use to see the effects of blowing, for example fans, feathers, cotton balls, paper, blocks of wood, and so forth. Because the teacher has not spent a significant amount of time setting up every area, it is much easier to find the energy and flexibility to put aside her or his own plans.

Again, a theme is a theme. We know that the intent is not that the children will hear "The Three Little Pigs" and go to centers and learn everything there is to know about pigs. Rather, it is essential that young children develop all of the skills that a child-negotiated and emergent curriculum promotes (DiCarlo & Vagianos, 2009). Denise could have created carnival centers in her classroom with games she had made and activities for literacy and art that she had created. While Denise's ideas may have been enticing to the children, they would still have been her ideas, coming from her, and given from her to the children to use. Many parents and educators chose these roles of parenting and teaching because they relish opportunities to use their creative energies and talents to engage with young children. Through a child-negotiated and emergent curriculum, the children also get to feel the excitement, creativity, and energy of creating the curriculum along with the adults (DiCarlo & Vagianos, 2009).

EMBEDDING LEARNING GOALS AND OBJECTIVES INTO AN EMERGENT CURRICULUM

Let's look specifically at how we may embed learning goals and objectives into an emergent curriculum. Let's think back to our carnival vignette one more time. The children's great carnival ideas motivated them to:

- develop an idea and a plan
- analyze the effectiveness of their plan
- persevere as they tested, retested, and experimented with their materials once again
- communicate their ideas, wants, needs, and thanks to others through communication with intent, drawing, and note-writing
- hone fine motor skills as they drew plans, constructed games, and wrote letters and posters

- problem-solve as they tested materials; readied their games, snacks, instruments, or prizes; and ran their booth for peers during the carnival
- give to the greater community

Again, a theme is a theme. Whether it emerges solely from an interest that the children share or in conjunction with ideas found in a theme-based curriculum, the key is to let the children communicate their intentions and plans for the learning that happens through a project. The Carnival Project theme certainly developed from the children's ideas. What research is demonstrating, and what we have experienced over and over again in our own classrooms, is that letting the learning themes emerge from the children's interests validates their interests, pulls from their strengths to meet their challenges, and promotes functional skill development within the routines of their lives (Angell et al., 2010; Casey & McWilliam, 2007; DiCarlo & Vagianos, 2009; Ganz & Flores, 2010; Harte, 2009; Jung, 2007; Koenig et al., 2009; National Research Council Institute of Medicine, 2000). As evidenced by our list of skills that the children developed or honed during the creation of and the communication around the carnival, we can embed skill development in all domains of learning at all levels when we follow or combine the various interests of the children. The multiple aspects of putting on a carnival offered opportunities for engaging skill development to many of the children in our school. As noted, in the carnival project, when we invited our youngest children to dance to our oldest children's rock band; when we invited other groups to cut, chop, and churn snacks; or when we allowed others to decide and create prizes and posters that people would love to win and see, every child had an opportunity to be an active decision-maker, creator, problem-solver, and participant.

Teachers can create plans that will capture the intentions of the children, provoke inquiry through providing materials and activities, facilitate the children's plans, embed learning opportunities to address each child's specific goals and objectives, and collect data and take notes on how well these objectives are met.

In addition, as evidenced by the carnival project, when the learning themes are driven by their interests, the children are actively engaged and motivated to behave in ways that allow them to participate (Angell et al., 2010; Casey & McWilliam, 2007; DiCarlo & Vagianos, 2009; Harte, 2009; Koenig et al., 2009). As previously mentioned, the children in the carnival project were purposely chosen because they were struggling to be interested by the materials and projects currently emerging in our class and they found interacting and working with their peers to be a challenge. Their interest and enthusiasm in creating a carnival fueled their intent to engage and interact even when the "work" of engaging and interacting to create the carnival felt challenging.

Imagining great ideas, communicating those ideas to others, thinking through plans for those ideas, co-constructing and problem-solving with others to create what has been planned, and referring to and collaborating with others to bring these ideas to life—these are the possibilities with young children! An emergent project approach affords young children engaging opportunities to hone and employ their developing rote and higher-level thinking skills with their peers, family members, therapists, and teachers. Through an emergent project approach, the captivating ideas of young children are heard and respected. The strengths of each young child are honored and celebrated.

PLANNING WITHIN A PROJECT-BASED CURRICULUM

As we begin to look at the process of teaching young children in a project-based approach it is vital to consider this as a journey in developing and learning. This journey is a process in and of itself. Why ascribe special significance to such a consideration? The answer is both simple and vital. If we consider this as a process, we give ourselves permission to take a breath and allow ourselves the experience of learning along with our students. The majority of the time, our learning will be different from the children's, yet we are still in a learning process. However, while implementing a project-based curriculum, you will find yourself learning about some interesting facts and processes right alongside the children.

This attitude allows educators the freedom to:

- Reconnect with their own wonderment and curiosity
- Model inquisitiveness and a quest for experiences and information
- Broaden their teaching practices to regularly include exploration, experimentation, research, and trial and error
- Embed teaching strategies into novel experiences and opportunities for young children
- Flexibly create opportunities and activities that promote the children's goals and objectives as they pursue their interests
- Use each child's strengths to drive the development of skills that have been challenging to him or her
- Focus on the process of engaging and creating rather than creating a specific product
- Balance providing opportunities for children to follow directions without dwelling on sending home or displaying worksheets and artwork that are all uniform and identical

This view of learning allows children the freedom to:

- Regulate their emotions and senses as an initial and integral part of learning
- Discover how they best learn from and process experiences
- Initiate and engage in an emergent curriculum that results from their own great ideas

- Develop a sense of belonging to a group
- Develop the lifelong skills of problem-solving and self-initiation around learning experiences
- Increase their self-esteem in developing cognitive skills in the manner that best fits their learning style
- Realize that life is full of learning opportunities
- Accept that failures and challenges are learning opportunities
- Relish that our daily routines offer incredible learning opportunities
- Confidently follow wonderment and interests throughout their lives

THE PLANNING PROCESS

Teachers and parents who are interested in an emergent or negotiated curriculum often ask: How do you involve children of differing abilities in the projects so that everyone is involved at their own skill or ability level? How do you infuse the objectives and skills into this type of curriculum? Projects are valid learning processes for all children regardless of ability. The project approach allows for multilevel instruction, which allows teachers to incorporate goals from each child's IEP within the exploration that occurs daily in the classroom Harris and Gleim (2008) state that "as young children work together, doing tasks that are suitable to their skills and interest, children become familiar and comfortable with diversity. . . . Many new opportunities, therefore, emerge for children to work collaboratively by embracing their differences and celebrating with new voices" (p. 33).

Planning for a project approach is not unlike planning for any type of theme-based unit: Teachers are still taking the opportunity to embed skills, concepts, and goals in the experiences planned for the class. The difference in more child-focused project planning is the need to be open to and reflective of the children's ideas and interests as they come up. In this chapter, two sample lesson plans will be presented. In the first one, a teacher-initiated lesson is introduced, but then the children are allowed to move that subject forward in response to their own interests in nursery rhymes and rhyming. In the second lesson plan, the teacher brings in materials as provocations in response to children's interests and to one child's challenges.

Ideally, objectives and goals are embedded in the learning that occurs on a daily basis and incorporated with the natural routines of the day, the children's play, provocations set up in the classroom, and the teacher's plans for the lesson.

Creating Lesson Plans from a Teacher-Initiated Project: Nursery Rhymes

In creating a nursery rhyme unit, the teacher, in addition to the daily reinforcement of concepts and skills, planned to specifically reinforce phonemic awareness, group cooperative play, sequencing, positional concepts, feelings/emotions, and extending rhymes to promote ideas. However, the children's interests and ideas took the lead in determining how the unit came to fruition. The children engaged in several different activities to illustrate the concepts, create their own rhymes and characters, and construct characters from their favorite nursery rhyme.

In addition, children were asked if they would like to make a bulletin board from their work around nursery rhymes. The children were excited at this prospect and voted on which nursery rhymes they would represent on the bulletin board. This voting process became an added objective for the class, which emphasized the concepts of one-to-one correspondence and rote counting. Once two nursery rhymes had been decided on, the children negotiated with one another and the teachers as to which part of the bulletin board each child would work on. Afterward, the children were asked to problem-solve on how to create their part of the board, which afforded the opportunity to reinforce fine motor skills.

In this particular scenario the teacher, rather than the children, initiated this unit of study, yet the children were allowed to direct the progression of the unit. Let's take a minute to reflect on how this unit might differ from a typical nursery rhyme unit. How was the bulletin board created? Rather than using an idea from a commercial book that provides both the idea and the template methods for creating the bulletin board, this board was decided on by the children. As a result, each child had some responsibility for deciding what the board would feature. This was accomplished through the process of generating suggestions of their favorite rhymes and then voting on which rhyme to feature. This created opportunities for social negotiations, counting, using one-to-one correspondence in a practical manner (each child gets one vote), and experiencing the practical implications of more and less. Once that decision was made each child had an opportunity to contribute to the board in his or her own unique manner, rather than having all the children complete the same pre-described product from a book. Some children constructed props from materials, such as the cat's fiddle, while others drew their own representation of the characters. While these representations might not be what we, as the adults in the classroom, had envisioned for the characters, the fact that the children were free to create and problem-solve such representations allows them the confidence and satisfaction of ownership of their work. This sense of ownership provides children with the confidence to think creatively on their own and generate new ideas.

Flexibility in Planning

In order to provide this flexibility, the lesson plans for the week must be fluid and include room for change during the week. Table 6.1 demonstrates a sample lesson plan for this type of lesson. As you can see in the lesson plan, many of the children's objectives are naturally occurring during the routine times of the day. Plans toward the end of the week were added in response to children's interests.

(text continues on page 117)

Table 6.1. Lesson Plan for Nursery Rhyme Unit

Goals Addressed:	Notes	Time	Monday	Tuesday	Wednesday	Thursday	Friday
Care of personal belongings: ES, DH, RG, NG Self-help skills, personal responsibility: hanging up backpack and coat with decreasing verbal, visual prompts: JM, BH, ES, DH, R, GE Greeting peers: JM ,ES Clean up, follow directions: JM, RG, ES,DH	Arrival Sign-in sheet & modified sign-in	9:00–9:15	Arrival	Arrival Provocation: Nursery rhyme ball available	Arrival	Arrival Provocation: Plastic eggs	Arrival Provocation: Limited # of musical instruments
Follow procedures group activities: BH, ES, DH, RG, JM Play & conversational skills w/ peer, take turns in conversations, sharing items: AC, ES, BH, JM Personal info name, age, gender Answer questions about self: DH Imitation facial gestures: JM, ES	Attendance Calendar Concept skills	9:15–9:40	Nursery rhyme ball for intro to unit: Objectives: Rhyme Imitation Taking turns Naming peers	Flannel board with nursery rhyme pictures: Hey Diddle, Diddle; Black Sheep; & Humpty Dumpty Objectives: Vocabulary (name objects) Memory of text Positional concepts Sequencing of story, rhymes Rote counting Number 3	Discuss bulletin board ideas G. wonders how tall a wall would have to be to break an egg, suggests we bring in eggs. Teacher suggests we talk more about it in small group,	Children explore what to fill eggs with so they will break open. Palette: Feathers, Legos, rocks, cotton balls N. begins using the bee and singing, add There Was a Little Bumble Bee to nursery rhymes	Music and Movement: Moving to nursery rhymes & keeping the beat with rhythm sticks
Understand dangers in environment: JM, ES	Resource	9:40–10:00	Day 6 Music	Day 1 Library	RESOURCE Day 2 No Resource	Day 3 PE	Day 4 PE

Strengths/Objectives		Time					
Personal space, rights of others: BH, ES, DH Follow 2-step direction: ES, BH, DH, RG, NG	AM Planning circle	10:00–10:15	Share ideas Choose centers	Share ideas Choose centers Children share ideas about making their own nursery rhymes Taking turns Attention to & engagement in large group Practice rhyming sounds	Share ideas Choose centers Discuss G's idea of using eggs. What would happen if we use real eggs? Suggests we stuff plastic eggs	Share ideas Choose centers Sign up to build and drop eggs	Share ideas Choose centers Sign up to build and drop eggs
Personal space, rights of others, personal info: BM, ES What to do in situations, use of objects: BH, ES, JM Respond to one & one more: JM Take turns in conversations, sharing items: BH, ES, AC, JM Initiate play, plan w/ peers, imaginative play: BH, ES, AC, Taking turns games w/ peers: JM,ES,BH, DH Matching colors or shapes: JM, ES, DH, NG Respond to peers, adults, directives, follow rules & routines, steps of task, work to completion time engaged in group activities: BH, ES, JM, RG	Centers, Snack	10:15–11:00	1. Book area: Flannel board with nursery rhymes (through the week) 2. Writing area: Nursery rhyme stampers (through the week) 3. Block area: Open ended with play characters added (3 pigs, bears, etc.) 4. Art area: Open ended materials offered 5. Variety of puzzles	6. Make sheep with open ended materials in art: Pom-poms, cotton ball, paint, oval cutouts, buttons, craft sticks. Reinforce textures, oval shape, color black, fine motor skills Repeat number 3 Continue with: 1, 2, & 5 3 continued: Farm animals added to block area The Hungry Thing book added to book area	7. Children work in small groups to make nursery rhyme stories. Obj.: Pre-writing, writing, dictation, negotiation w/ peers Continue with 1, 2, 3, 6 (for children who did not finish art)	Children work with Miss J. in art to represent "Hey Diddle, Diddle" for bulletin board Small Group experiments with Miss D at the block area with plastic eggs filled with different materials Book area: Change to listening songs and books	N. makes bee for bulletin board: Identify color of yellow Textures: Rough and soft Continue with bulletin board Small group in blocks, etc.

Table 6.1. Lesson Plan for Nursery Rhyme (*continued*)

Goals Addressed:	Notes	Time	Monday	Tuesday	Wednesday	Thursday	Friday
Initiating play, planning with peers, and engaging in imaginative play with peers: BH, ES, DH, RG	Outside	11:10–11:40	Outside	Outside	Outside	Outside	Outside
Washing hands, independent toileting: DH RG, JM Waiting in line: BH, ES, RG Dressing independently: ES, DH, NL	Prep for lunch Hand-washing	11:40–11:50	Pottying for JM, ES	Pottying for JM, ES	Pottying for JM, ES	Pottying for JM, ES	Pottying for JM, ES
Greet peers, adults: BH, ES, DH, RG, JM Respond to name: JM, ES Ask for help when needed: JM No overstuffing mouth, use utensils: NG, ES Drink from unlidded cup: NG Wash hands: BH, ES Ask for food or drink w/ words, gestures: JM, ES, NG		11:50–12:30	Lunch & clean up	Lunch & clean up	Lunch & clean up	Lunch	Lunch
Answer questions demonstrate understanding of what to do in situations & understand the use of objects: BH, ES, DH, RG Classification and positional concepts: DH, RG Literacy activities in a large group setting: DH, RG	Pre-K literacy Math concepts	12:30–1:00	Rhyming game Reading of the book *The Hungry Thing*	Favorite rhyme chart for voting Objectives: Answer yes, no One-to-one correspondence Rote counting, more and less	Intro to letter H Letter H songs	Which nursery rhyme has "H" in it? What other words have "H" sound?	

Creating Lesson Plans from a Child-Initiated Project: Superheroes!

When working with curriculum that has emerged from children's interests, the planning is more open-ended from the start, with provocations and set-up of materials as the primary form of planning. Again, many of the goals and objectives are covered through the daily routines.

Thomas, a child in Debbie's class, was bright and had good ideas, but was very hesitant to take risks of any sort. This affected his development in personal-social, adaptive (in the form of engagement and initiative), language reasoning, and problem-solving abilities. Thomas was a child who did not volunteer information at circle or attempt to make conjectures or predictions, which seemed to be an outcome of his hesitancy with taking risks. He wasn't yet settling himself into meaningful play, which also seemed to be a result of this hesitancy. Thomas had been observed with other children in the block area, but he would only handle a few blocks and quickly leave the area if his block towers fell down.

What Thomas did like, however, was Batman. In fact, he was passionate about everything that had to do with Batman! Despite the natural teacher response that superheroes and all that goes with that genre remain at home, Debbie could not deny the potential of bringing in something about which Thomas was this passionate. In order to not assume or promote any gender stereotypes, some female superheroes were added to the materials in the classroom.

Debbie's initial plan was to bring in the superheroes as a provocation and let the children have some time to play with them freely (see Figure 6.5). At the same time, a pulley was set up in the block area as a second provocation, to encourage problem-solving skills.

After a short period of time, Debbie asked the children if they would like to sign up to play with the superheroes. Of course, there was no shortage of eager participants. However, there was a condition for playing with the superheroes: The superheroes definitely needed a house to play in, and anyone who was going to play with them needed to help build a house. Ahhh—the power of intentionality! Even though Thomas was unsure about how to go about this, he was very willing to stay and work on it in order to have a turn with Batman! A friend named Jessie collaborated with Thomas, and they soon had created a livable space for their superheroes (see Figure 6.6).

Once Thomas had persevered long enough to learn the basics of building, he came to realize that he was actually quite good at it. Thus began a year-long process of teaching Thomas the most important thing he needed to learn at this point in his young life: It's okay to take risks.

The superhero project took on a life of its own at that point. As children eagerly discussed what kind of superhero they would like to be and what powers they would like to have, puppet-making materials were made available, and children worked one-on-one with Miss Judy to make puppets of themselves as superheroes. Their ideas varied from a "Super Star girl who can push her star and go to the stars" to a "Super guy that has a net that picks up and throws stuff in the water and then gets it out!"

Figure 6.5.
Playing with
Superheroes

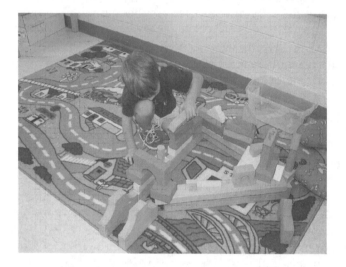

Figure 6.6.
Building a
Superhero
House

The process of making superhero puppets entailed fine motor skill development, making choices, vocabulary development, making up stories, and much, much more. This activity eventually grew into making a life-sized superhero, which involved measuring, color identification, shape identification, voting, graphs, and more (see Figure 6.7).

Eventually, one of the children noticed the pulley in the art area. At that point there was an increased opportunity for problem-solving and cooperative play, which brought Thomas's personal-social skills to a new level. It also inspired a lot of flying superheroes!

The lesson plan for this project looks different in some ways than the lesson plan that began as a teacher-initiated plan (see Table 6.2). The primary planning at the beginning of the week was the provocation of the superheroes

Figure 6.7. Drawing a Superhero

and the building of the superhero house. This project lasted several weeks, and though the planning for the life-sized superhero was not on this plan, the plan was fluid, with plenty of open-ended space to add particular activities as the project went along.

SUMMARY

Even in a more emergent, interests-based curriculum, the teacher must be continuously planning. Yet, the most striking difference is that interest-based plans are generated in a more collaborative manner with the children in the classroom using the children's interests as the springboard for ideas and activities. At times, the ideas come directly from the children's interests, such as the pirate scenario in Chapter 1. At other times, the teacher may initiate a unit of study, such as farms. However, in an interest-based curriculum, the teacher's goal is to become very cognizant of the children and to relate what the children are most interested in to that unit of study.

Planning in this manner necessitates that we become reflective teachers and that we take the time at the end of the day to ask ourselves and those working with us some important questions. What are the children really interested in? How can we take that interest and further their development, skills, and concepts? What do they want to know more about? What is it that may be impeding this child in moving forward? What child in the class might facilitate that movement? The list can go on and on, but this reflection is the part of teaching that can be creative, motivating, and exciting. To borrow a phrase from James Taylor, "That's why I'm here!"

Table 6.2. Superhero Lesson Plan

Goals Addressed:	Notes	Time	Monday	Tuesday	Wednesday	Thursday	Friday
Care of personal belongings: ES, DH, RG, NG Self-help skills, personal responsibility: hanging up backpack and coat with decreasing verbal/visual prompts: JM, BH, ES, DH, RG, GE Greeting peers: JM, ES Clean up, follow directions JM, RG, ES, DH	Arrival Sign-in sheet/ modified sign-in sheet	9:00–9:15	Arrival Superheroes in circle and art area	Arrival Tables with scissors and pictures of superheroes to cut out	Arrival Repeat Tuesday	Arrival Provocation: Batman on pulley	Arrival
Follow procedures in group activities: BH, ES, DH, RG, JM Play & conversational skills w/ peer, take turns in conversations, sharing items: AC, ES, BH, JM Personal info (name, age, gender) Answer questions about self: DH Imitate facial gestures: JM, ES	Attendance Calendar Concept skills	9:15–9:40	Question: Which is your favorite superhero?	Review of building: What kind of house did you make? What kind of rooms? What are they used for? How will you change it today?	C says she would like to make her own superhero; discussion follows	One-to-one correspondence: How many capes would we need if every child could fly?	What have superheroes been doing in the block area with the people? Begin a story line
Understand dangers in environment JM, ES	Resource	9:40–10:00	RESOURCE				
			Day 6 Music	Day 1 Library	Day 2 No resource	Day 3 PE	Day 4 PE

Objectives		Time	Monday				Friday
Personal space, rights of others: BH, ES, DH Follow two-step direction: ES, BH, DH, RG, NG	AM Planning circle	10:00–10:15	Share ideas Choose centers Announce that in order to play superhero they will need a house to be their headquarters Sign up for superhero	Share ideas Choose centers Sign up for superhero play	Share ideas Choose centers Children make a list of what their own superheroes might do	Share ideas Choose centers Sign up to make puppets Discussion about Batman on pulley	Share ideas Choose centers Create a small group to make superhero story with puppets made so far
Personal space/rights of others, personal info: BM, ES What to do in situations/ use of objects: BH, ES, JM Respond to one & one more: JM Take turns, t/t in conversations/sharing items: BH, ES, AC, JM Initiate play, plan w/ peers, imaginative play: BH, ES, AC Taking turns, games w/ peers: JM, ES, BH, DH Matching colors or shapes: JM, ES, DH, NG Respond to peers/adults, directives, follow rules & routines, steps of task, work to completion, time engaged in group activities: BH, ES, JM, RG	Centers, Snack	10:15–11:00	1. Provocation in block area of pulley and blocks for house 2. Open-ended art 3. Open-ended manipulatives 4. Book corner with superhero books 5. Writing area with superhero stickers	1 repeated 2 repeated 6. Potato heads with material and paper for capes, masks, with tape available 7. Dress-up area: capes, loose material for creating costumes Art area: Paper, scissors, tape, string to facilitate making costumes 4 repeated 5 repeated	8. Materials added to the art area to create puppets. Children work with Miss Judy to decide what their superhero will look like Block area: children add people for the superheroes to catch and save (document stories) 7 repeated NL- colors for costumes-matching	7 continued 8 continued 9. Facilitate small-group learning about the pulley 3 repeated 10. Writing area with names of superheroes and pictures that were cut out at the beginning of the week	Small group for story 8 continued 9 continued 3 repeated 10 repeated

Table 6.2. Superhero Lesson Plan (*continued*)

Goals Addressed:	Notes	Time	Monday	Tuesday	Wednesday	Thursday	Friday
Initiating play, planning with peers, and engaging in imaginative play with peers: BH, ES, DH, RG	Outside	*11:10–11:40*	Outside	Outside	Outside	Outside	Outside
Washing hands, independent toileting: DH, RG, JM Waiting in line: BH, ES, RG Dressing independently: ES, DH	Prep for lunch Hand washing	*11:40–11:50*					
Greet peers/adults: BH, ES, DH, RG, JM Respond to name: JM, ES Ask for help when needed: JM No overstuffing mouth, use utensils: NG, ES Drink from unlidded cup: NG Wash hands: BH, ES Ask for food or drink w/ words, gestures: JM, ES, NG		*11:50–12:30*	Lunch & clean up	Lunch & clean up	Lunch & clean up	Lunch & clean up	Lunch & clean up
Answer questions, demonstrate understanding of what to do in situations, & understand the use of objects: BH, ES, DH, RG Classification and positional concepts: DH, RG Literacy activities in a large-group setting: DH, RG	Pre-K literacy Math concepts	*12:30–1:00*	Introduction of letter S Does it sound like flying? What else does it sound like?	Letter S song What kind of superhero would you be?	Quantitative and opposite Using figures: Short/tall Big/little Fast/slow, etc.	B suggests making a superhero song, generate rhyming words	Finish up song

CHAPTER 7

Processing Strengths-Based IEPs

We educators and therapists often approach IEP season, eligibilities, and annual reviews with dread, knowing that we will spend countless hours assessing, scoring assessments, and drafting Present Levels of Academic Achievement and Functional Performance (PLAAFP) reports, goals, and objectives. Yet, we value the information that accurate assessments and detailed reports contribute toward the creation of learning experiences for young children with special rights (Capizzi, 2008).

What becomes overwhelming, however, is the reality that these responsibilities are often in addition to what we simultaneously are managing: planning, gathering of materials and provocations, setting up the classroom environment, creating learning groups, teaching small groups, working on projects with the kids, teaching circles, collecting data, and completing interim progress reports and narratives, report cards, and 9-week progress reports and narratives. We must juggle these demands of teaching while maintaining undivided focus on accurately conducting assessments, writing reports, and drafting IEPs (Carter et al., 2010).

Our participation in the Eligibility Meetings, our need to conduct the Annual Reviews, and our facilitation of the IEP Meetings further tax our time. Our role in these meetings requires us to use our expertise in child development and special education services to, at times, broker what the family wants for their child, what we have determined the child needs, and what the school district or system provides. There is no doubt that report-writing responsibilities and participation in mandated meetings in early childhood special education are time-consuming and energy-draining.

SEEING THE PROCESS THROUGH PARENTS' EYES

Yet, imagine for a moment what it must be like for the families to attend these meetings about their very young child. At the child's young age, this is often the first experience that families have with the IEP process. They enter a conference room with a table full of administrators, therapists, and educators all seated with their reports in hand. Imagine hearing the agenda for the meeting, which is full of educational jargon, most, if not all, of which sounds like a foreign language. Next, they are offered an additional copy of their rights as the parents in this legally mandated process. The word "rights" might strike additional nerves, further increasing their anxiety. As they sit there appearing to process all that is being reported, their brains might be thinking, "Will I have to fight for my child's rights? Will I have to defend my child's rights? Am I prepared and qualified to do this? How will I be sure that my child will receive all that she rightly deserves?" Unnerving, overwhelming, and daunting, to say the least. And all of this is before you even begin to discuss your child's educational plan!

Further, imagine that the first thing the group discusses is all of your child's developmental deficits. As each member of the panel reads the reports about your child's PLAAFP you hear, "Not able to, Does not, Cannot, Below average, Delayed, etc." Families know that their child is delayed and below average. Chances are they also have been hearing it from relatives, neighbors, and day care or preschool teachers. What families want to know and to plan for during these meetings is what to do to help their child. Families often will ask, "My child is already behind, how will he ever catch up?"

CONDUCTING AUTHENTIC ASSESSMENTS

Just as we create the school environment to listen and respond to the interests and emotional and social connections of the children at the beginning of the year, it is essential to offer the same to the families during the assessment and IEP development processes (Shannon, 2004). Whether evaluating each child for eligibility of services or assessing for IEP development, school districts typically use commercially produced norm-referenced evaluations and criterion-referenced assessments respectively. It is crucial to confirm that each testing tool, environment, and evaluator meets the critical principles of effective assessment as described by Bricker (2004):

- Familiar evaluators administer the tools in a familiar environment for the child.
- The testing tools reflect the developmentally appropriate curricular content of the interventions.
- The developmentally sequenced assessment items serve as benchmarks for planning intervention.
- The assessment tools are normed and field-validated for the child, whether typically developing or presenting with disabilities. The tool must encourage and score for accommodations to meet the child's testing needs. (Bricker, 2002, p. 15)

Many of these tools call for the assessor to interview and/or conference with the family in order to learn from them as the experts on their child. This provides the perfect opportunity to connect with each family in ways that demonstrate the school's genuine intent to form a partnership (Cheatham & Ostrosky, 2009; Hollingsworth et al., 2009; Turnbull et al., 2006).

Very young children will feel more comfortable when assessments take place in a familiar setting, such as their home or day care setting. The home provides opportunities for the assessor to ask family members about the child's skills and to observe the child's skills and environment firsthand. The assessor can interact and conduct the parent report sections of the assessment with the family (Bricker, Clifford, Yovanaoff, Pretti-Frontczak, Waddell, Allen, & Hoselton, 2008). This allows the child to observe the assessor, who may be a complete stranger, engaging with the family in a friendly conversational tone. The family's ease and comfort with the assessor will promote the same reaction in the child.

Often, schools will ask that family members bring preschool-age children to be assessed in the school setting. Again, create a moment to converse with the family in front of the child before asking the child to go with you to an assessment room. By seeing and hearing that the family comfortably connects with the assessor, the child will be more willing to do so also. If the child is uncomfortable leaving the family, invite the family to join you in the assessment room. Share with the family any guidelines they should know, such as not prompting the child to answer the assessment questions.

In addition to parent reports, if the child is already receiving services, include the authentic assessments conducted during the school year, such as the portfolios of the children's work and data collection during their project, small-group, and guided play. These offer a wealth of data and information that truly describes who each young child is, highlighting his or her strengths of multiple intelligences, learning styles, interests, preferences, and skills (Morrison, 1999). Use this holistic portrait to draft eligibility, IEP, and triennial reports that accentuate the strengths of each child as the team plans to move her development forward (Gischlar, Hojnoski, & Missal, 2009; Hollingsworth et al., 2009).

CREATING AN AUTHENTIC PLAAFP

Once the holistic assessment has been completed, it is time to draft the section on the child's PLAAFP. Start each report and PLAAFP with the child's family and strengths (Capizzi, 2008; Jung, 2008). Acknowledge that the child is a member of the family and note the number of siblings and relationships of the other members in the home. These family members comprise the team working with the child within the home and community (Trent-Stainbrook, Kaiser, & Frey, 2007). Ask the family what they enjoy together at home and in the community. These activities might range from various hobbies, genres of movies or storybooks, and favorite sports, to going to worship, going out to eat in local restaurants, or visiting theme parks. Include these insights, as they speak to who the child is within the dynamics of the family and community (Hollingsworth et al., 2009; Jung, 2008; Mitchell & Hauser-Cram, 2009).

Reviewing the parent interview data from the assessments, educators and therapists may be faced with a list of delays or deficits the families want to address. The families might say, "My child can't eat, use the toilet, or take a bath without a struggle." "My child won't sit through a storybook or a movie with the family." "My child doesn't stop hurting us because he is always angry about something." "My child can't even name colors, and she is 4 years old."

Continue your commitment to accentuating the strengths of each child as you draft the PLAAFP, with a positive and holistic perspective of the child. We can set the tone in our IEP-writing meetings that every child has the potential of their many strengths, and that the team should plan to use those strengths to further the child's development.

Describing the delays and deficits that the families want addressed not only focuses on the challenges of the child, but it also insinuates that the family has a passive role. The family's role is not merely to share the delays that they want the school system to address, but to be an active member of the child's team. We have to empower family members with the knowledge that they will need to carry out the therapies and interventions all of the hours and days in which the child is not in school (Hollingsworth et al., 2009; Jung, Gomez, Baird, & Keramidas, 2008; Sandall et al., 2005).

Think positively and progressively. Approach the section of the report that will include the family's input by writing the family's hopes for the child in planning the educational program. When we hear from the family about what they enjoy together at home and in the community, we can then ask, "What do you hope your child will be able to begin to do with the family?" Families might say, "Eat, toilet, allow a bath." "Sit through a storybook or movie." "Communicate strong feelings." "Enjoy playing with siblings." "Name colors, shapes, letters, and numbers." Then the family and the other team members will begin to think dynamically in terms of the child progressing, developing, and interacting. These hopes, along with additional developmental skills noted by the educators and therapists in the PLAAFP, will form the working goals and objectives in the IEP (Hollingsworth et al., 2009). Andrea Capizzi asserts that "PLAAFP should be stated positively, focusing on what a student is able to do rather than what a student cannot do. The primary purpose of PLAAFP is to provide a place from which to start teaching the student" (Capizzi, 2008, p. 23).

STRENGTHS-BASED APPROACHES TO CREATING A COLLABORATIVE TEAM

Below is an example of how a PLAAFP that focuses on the child's strengths might read. As you read, imagine the smiles and nods of recognition that will erupt among those attending the meeting as they begin to form a genuine picture of this child. Imagine the pride the family will feel when the meeting starts with their story and all that they do with and for their children. Imagine the encouragement that the administration, therapists, and educators will feel when they meet this family, share their mutual appreciation for the child, and begin to develop a collaborative relationship as members of the child's team.

Sample Strengths-Based PLAAFP

Herschel is a 3-year-old boy who lives with his parents, three older sisters, and two older brothers. His mother reports that Herschel loves to be physically active. He runs, climbs, and jumps as often as he can. He chooses to wrestle with his older brothers. He builds forts with the couch cushions so that he can burrow under the large pillows. He rarely chooses quiet time, but when his parents ask to be alone, he will work on a large floor puzzle, hammer and shape play dough, or drive his trucks around the rug. His mother noted that Herschel has always enjoyed drumming, tapping beats, chanting, and singing. The family enjoys going for long walks within their neighborhood, working in their vegetable garden, having cookouts with their neighbors, and watching movies or reading storybooks as a family. Herschel's mother hopes that Herschel will be able to play and share his toys with the children from the neighborhood when they visit. She hopes that Herschel will be able to sit and listen to storybooks when they read to him, and that he will be able to tell the family with words when something is bothering him. The family plays his favorite musical CD to calm him when he is unable to soothe himself or be soothed by another.

The PLAAFP, which introduces the team to the child's strengths, will also include the results of the initial evaluation or most recent assessments. Again, set the tone for the meeting and for the child's educational program by starting with the strengths. For example, if your school system notes the child's current performance in each developmental domain, start with the child's strengths in each domain. Include:

- What the family reports that the child is demonstrating at home
- The skills the child demonstrated on the formal evaluations
- What the child was able to accomplish on current assessments
- If the child has been in your class, note the skills the child has demonstrated during the authentic assessments and data collection that you have conducted throughout the year

Starting with and including the child's strengths in each domain informs everyone about what the child is capable of as a learner. It is important to distinguish the skills in each domain that the child has mastered, those that are emerging, and those that the child will be working toward. By sequencing the skills development within each domain, the transdisciplinary team can discuss the order in which skills are acquired, that evidence shows we do not skip skills along the way to catch up to our peers, and, more importantly, that the child's development of foundational skills will lead to meeting the goals through the noted mastered and emerging objectives. This often proves informative again when we are writing the narratives for the interim and 9-week reports through which we highlight the child's progress toward meeting her or his individual IEP goals.

The section on the child's evaluation and assessment results of the PLAAFP report might read like this:

> The Named Assessment Tool, parent report, and teacher observation and data collection indicate that Herschel has mastered the following:
>
> Adaptive (Self-help) Skills: Herschel is caring for his belongings and independently carrying and unzipping his lunchbox and backpack. Herschel is able to independently eat finger foods and drink from a lidded cup. In the sub-area of undressing and dressing, Herschel is able to independently undress and to pull up pants without fasteners.
>
> Emerging Adaptive Skills: Using the toilet, and turning the faucet on and off when prompted by an adult to begin the hand-washing process; drinking from an unlidded cup and using a spoon with minimal spillage; and is beginning to unfasten snaps and zippers on the front of his clothing.
>
> Herschel will work toward developing skills in putting his belongings away, pulling on over-the-head shirts, initiating use of the toilet, independently washing his hands after toileting.

This format then continues for each developmental domain. Some school systems will use the format in which the assessor bullets each set of skills under subheadings, such as Mastered Skills, Emerging Skills, and Goal Skills. The emerging skills and the skills that the child needs to develop then become the goals on the IEP.

The narratives that we write for every interim report and every 9-week report card could and should include the same information, based upon the child's demonstrated strengths. Here conversations and conferences with families, teacher observation and data collection, and authentic assessments comprise what is shared in the narratives (Gischlar et al., 2009). Focusing on the strengths of each child throughout the narratives, educators and therapists are able to promote a transdisciplinary approach by informing all of the interventions and strategies that have been successful for the child and those that did not meet the child's needs in that setting. All members of the transdisciplinary team will have the written narratives describing the interventions used by each member to refer to as they try those interventions with the child in other settings (Block & Chandler, 2005; Kemmis & Dunn, 1996; Olson, Murphy, & Olson, 1999; Shannon, 2004). These narrative records provide a historical perspective, not only for those working with the child this year, but also for future educators and therapists.

Sample Strengths-Based Narrative

Below is a sample of a strengths-based narrative:

> Herschel has made notable progress in his Adaptive Skills development during these first 9 weeks. Upon arrival, he independently carries his backpack to the class. When he watches the other children unpack, he will independently unpack his backpack. When he notices the materials on the tables beyond the coat area, he will drop his backpack and go to use the morning work items. With one or two gestural cues from the teacher to follow the mounted picture schedule for unpacking, which is in his view between the coat area and the morning work tables, Herschel is able to unpack first and then use the morning work materials. Herschel independently refers to an identical unpacking schedule mounted next to his cubby to unpack to completion. Herschel has been able to follow visual picture cues to wash his hands. Herschel uses self-talk as he refers to the unpacking and hand-washing picture schedules. At the time this narrative was written, Herschel continued to need an adult to monitor his hand-washing and ensure that he began and thoroughly completed the process. As a class, we have begun singing a song that we wrote to chant while we wash our hands. Herschel has memorized the song and is beginning to follow the steps as he sings it while washing. Herschel has been able to successfully use both picture cues and chants to learn and follow the steps to completing new skills.

For each goal on the child's IEP, the narrative will continue describing the interventions and strategies used, the progress the child is making, and possible uses for the interventions and strategies in other settings, especially the home and community

Through such a narrative, you can ensure to set a respectful and hopeful tone for the family and for our colleagues with the wording you choose and the order in which you present the results in the reports. By breaking the child's skills into those that have been recently mastered, those that are emerging, and those that the child will work on next, you emphasize the child's strengths and potential.

The information included in the eligibility, PLAAFP, narrative, and 9-week reports is essential in promoting a transdisciplinary approach to each child's education. A transdisciplinary approach is the goal. The team plans to:

- Create a communication system that works for everyone on the team and to which everyone will have access
- Instruct one another on strategies and techniques and how to use them to support the development of the child whether at school, home, or in the community.

Let the feelings of dread around conducting the assessments and writing the reports begin to be replaced with the satisfaction of connecting with the family and building a well-informed foundation for supporting and promoting the development of each child.

COLLABORATIVE TEAMS DOCUMENTING AND COLLECTING DATA

Observing and recording observations allows teachers to genuinely come to know each child at the beginning of the year, as discussed in Chapter 3. When we begin to put those observations to use, we create learning environments, groupings of children, and projects to promote each child's development. By documenting each child's work within these areas, groups, and projects, we collect authentic data about skills development. This collection of data informs the educators' work with the children at school, but also the families as they work with their children at home and in the community. So, how do we collect authentic work samples from such young children?

When we follow a child-negotiated and emergent curriculum, we have less teacher-directed paper products than we might have with traditional preschool cut-and-paste tasks. What we have instead is a wealth of data truly representing each child. The children's plan for their learning is available, as well as any notes they write requesting materials or support from others; any text they dictate or write for plays, shows, or dramatic play; and any photographs or video footage taken of interactions, large-scale, or kinesthetic work samples such as buildings from blocks, groups interacting on the playground, or constructing carnival games. All of the work embedded in the routines of the school, the play of the children, the small learning groups, the project groups, and the playground may be represented.

DOCUMENTATION AND DATA COLLECTION FOR AUTHENTIC ASSESSMENTS

Becoming more common in school settings, portfolios are viable tools for organizing and presenting samples of embedded learning within the routines, play, project groups, and teacher-directed activities. Creating portfolios allows a chronological look at each child's skills progression for the educators and for each family. Even with the technological potential to create electronic portfolios for each child, teachers may continue to bind hard copies. Recalling that some families do not have access to computers or internet services, creating bound copies may work better in these incidences. Often teachers will use three-ring binders with page protectors to hold the paper samples, photos, CDs of favorite songs, or whatever other types of work are created throughout the year (Morrison, 1999; Vakil et al., 2003).

This assembled collection documents the capacity of each child's skills and, more important, each child's interests, preferences, thought processes, and problem-solving abilities. Documentation begins to represent the essence of who the child is and the potential of the child's capabilities. The compilation of data from formal evaluations, parent reports, informal assessments, teacher observations, and portfolio samples provides a complete portrait of the child's aptitude. These data then serve to authenticate the results from which each child's transdisciplinary team will craft each Individualized Education Program.

SUMMARY

It does not matter if teams are writing initial IEPs for a young child who is newly eligible for the right to receive special education services or a young child whom the teacher has come to truly know throughout a school year. Strengths-based IEP and educational processes both open and close circles of development for children and their families. When a team's focus is on starting with the child's strengths, all of the members benefit from the process.

Starting IEP meetings by respectfully acknowledging the strengths of the children and their families sets the tone for subsequent interactions among families, educators, and school systems. Just as all children have strengths and competencies, so do all families. Despite the challenges they face by virtue of having young children with disabilities, families want to provide the best services for their children. As educators and school systems, we have the responsibility to listen to the families about what they want for their children. Then we may use our expertise in child development and best special educational practices to work with families to devise the learning goals and services for their children. We focus on the potential rather than the challenges when we base the individualized education plans on the strengths that the families and their children possess to meet their needs. This potential is what drives families and educators to collaborate as teams as they provide comprehensive support for the children's development.

Holding IEP meetings that begin by addressing the strengths of the children and their families positively affects the interactions of the families and the educators and the families and the school systems thereafter. The teams develop the sense that they have joined together to respectfully learn from and work with each other to keep the children's skills development progressing forward. This solid foundation will stand true as teams tackle challenges and difficult decisions through the process of the children's education.

CHAPTER 8

Growing Stronger Through a Strengths-Based Approach

In this chapter we will pull together the pieces of the strengths-based approach that we have offered throughout the book. We will focus on the enriching benefits of this approach. The benefits reach the children, their families, educators, school systems, and the community as a whole. Involving all in the strengths-based process ensures that everyone builds stronger relationships and gains from these relationships in many ways. By sharing their experience and expertise, the teachers, therapists, and family members may implement the strategies and interventions with the children continuously. The project approach as one aspect of the strengths-based process permits the adults to spend less time creating materials and art activities and more time embedding learning into their interactions with the children. Through this, the children and the adults learn from each other's strengths and develop to their fullest potential.

Historically, early childhood special education practices have focused on remediating the deficits, delays, and disabilities of young children receiving their services. Educators planned interventions that honed in on the specific skills that the children lacked, and planned tasks that gave them repeated practice with those skills. When the children's days were filled with the tasks that most challenged them, they developed the general conclusion that schoolwork was simply too difficult for them. We can imagine what that did to each child's self-esteem. The children had what they thought were great ideas. Yet, the expectation was that children were to follow the teacher's directions and do the tasks the teacher had planned. Thinking back to the vignette from Chapter 4 about Trent's first sustained interaction with his peers, he was able to sustain imaginative play with his peers by creating a whimsical, wooden-bead vegetable garden. Denise shared documentation of this emergent lesson with Trent's visiting special education teacher from the local school district. Denise told the teacher that Trent had initiated telling her about his pretend garden. He had then willingly talked to the other children about each "bead vegetable" growing there. More remarkably, Trent had laughed with friends as he used his humor to create silly vegetables growing in the garden. The special education teacher looked at the documentation as she listened to Denise's recount of the interaction. She then looked at Denise with a hint of disgust and shook her head. All she said about Trent's interaction with peers was, "How bizarre."

On another day, Denise observed a speech and language therapist who arrived at the school to work with Trent as he sat with a group of peers reading one of his favorite books. The therapist's plan for that session was to teach Trent to answer wh- questions, who, what, when, where, and why. She immediately told the other children to leave the area because she was there to work with Trent. She then asked Trent a series of wh- questions, a few of which were about the book and the rest were unrelated to what Trent had been doing. Later, while Trent was eating a snack, the therapist repeatedly asked him, "Trent, Trent, what is your name, Trent?" Trent turned and looked pleadingly at Denise, but did not respond to the question. The therapist repeated her question to Trent two more times without a response from him, so she stopped and wrote some notes in her notebook. Denise turned to Trent, saying, "Trent, I hear that Mrs. Smith knows your name, but I think that she wants you to say it for her." Trent swallowed his last bite of snack and said, "I know, Denise. But I am eating and I don't want to choke."

We as educators now know that best practice recommends embedding young children's learning into their routines and play interactions. Routines and play interactions are the naturally occurring and developmentally appropriate settings through which children explore, communicate, collaborate, and co-construct with peers and adults, and therefore learn. Today, most adults working with young children read the above scenario and recognize the potential of facilitating Trent's emerging social skills. Teachers and therapists might form small groups with Trent and a few peers. Their plans might include reading humorous books about the silly antics of animals or garden vegetables, or using humorous language cards that show cartoon drawings of common compound words, such as a sweating dog for hot dog—all of which the children would likely thoroughly enjoy.

Even with the progress we have made as professionals in creating developmentally appropriate learning groups and activities for young children, we consciously must continue to use caution when we approach our work with young children with special rights. As noted throughout this book, when we approach early childhood special education with the intent to give the children practice in completing the traditional academics of preschool, and exhibiting the behaviors of typically developing children in traditional school settings, we run the risk of limiting their potential. As with all children, children with special rights have unique learning styles and challenges, and require and deserve the consideration of how that impacts their learning and their own sense of creativity and accomplishment. When we ask young children with special rights to complete traditional, theme-driven tasks, their challenges may appear so significant that we miss the multitude and range of each child's strengths.

DISCOVERING THE CAPABILITIES BEHIND THE DISABILITIES

As educators, we look at children's skills and behaviors as developmental communicators. We observe and assess to determine where each child is developmentally, and then we plan how to bring each child to the next developmental level. This is the individualized intent of the IEP. The challenge is to not underestimate the children's capacities because we expect and often see the limitations of the delays. Rather, our mission is to discover the capabilities of each child that, at times, appear hidden behind the dis-abilities.

In thinking of these young children as children first, we know that they have intelligences, interests, skills, learning styles, preferences, and emotional connections that form their many individual strengths. When we learn from families about their children's strengths, we positively begin to forge strong relationships with the families as we learn how resilient, resourceful, creative, and engaged the children and their families are with each other. The children's relationship with their families is their primary strength. As we educators connect with families to learn from and share strategies with them, the support to the children grows exponentially. We create the strengths-based process by joining the experience of the family and the strategies of the educators so that the children receive comprehensive support of their development across all settings. Educators implement strategies in rich learning experiences at school. Families implement the strategies at home and in the greater community, all of the hours and days outside of school.

Whether writing IEPs for a child's initial eligibility to receive services or as an annual IEP, building strong relationships with the families may continue to be an intention. By basing each child's education plan on the strengths that she or he possesses, the educational team acknowledges the child's potential for meeting the goals. The team discusses services based upon this potential. Then the IEP is ready for implementation, with a clear understanding of each child's strengths that the team may use in the process of meeting the identified goals.

By pulling from children's strengths to meet their needs and to promote their development across all domains, we affirm for the children that they may call upon their capabilities, resilience, and relationships when facing novel and/or taxing situations. Their strengths support children in forming connections to the school environment and people. In giving time to listen to the families' wealth of experience and knowledge about their children's interests and preferences, educators may begin to create a school environment that speaks to those strengths even before the children arrive.

Arriving at a school that embraces their interests and many other strengths fosters the children's sense of belonging and attachment. Once the children securely connect with the adults and their peers at school, their strengths serve as emotional hooks providing intrinsic motivation to sustain their engagement as they meet developmental challenges. Children may develop avoidance or aversion behaviors toward skills that they find challenging. Yet, as we observed through the vignette about Mallory (Chapter 1), and many other vignettes throughout the book, by tapping into their strengths, children call upon their intrinsic motivation to face and meet developmental challenges. Educators guide children with recommended strategies and interventions, but the children own the intent to accomplish the tasks.

Just as educational team members relinquish their roles and follow one another's advice about strategies and interventions to use, through a strengths-based approach, educators become free to follow the children's lead in choosing topics to study. The discovery of each child's strengths, and the creation and use of a strengths-based approach, perpetually evolves as a process for the educators, as well as, the children. Educators must prepare to shift their thinking and pedagogical practices through the process of a strengths-based approach, but the benefits to all warrant those shifts.

The progression to using a strengths-based approach begins systemwide before the school year begins. The educational community commits to allocating ample time and resources to focus on getting to know the children's strengths and needs from the families, cumulative files, and colleagues. In realizing that along with peers and the adults, the environment is the third teacher, the intentions shift from decorating the school by the first day to choosing spaces and materials that will stir the interests and intelligences of the children. This may necessitate explaining the choice of materials or the emptiness of bulletin boards gracing the room, but once the children's work and the documentation of the process leading to the work are displayed, typically all can clearly see the benefits. A collaborative teacher described the few blank walls and bulletin boards in the class she shared with Denise as "a blank canvas" waiting for the exhibition of the children's learning.

When school systems follow a strengths-based approach, they will creatively afford for the staff to stay abreast of the latest recommended, evidence-based practices. This way, in aspiring to use a transdisciplinary approach, all team members will enter informed collaboration as they build cooperative relationships, share strategies and interventions, and plan for effective communication and scheduling. Beginning of the year lesson plans center on supporting the children to adjust to separating from family, the sensory input and expectations of the new environment, following the routines, and learning about the adults and peers who will share this school setting with them. This, too, calls upon school systems to allocate ample personnel and creatively scheduled phase-in periods to keep the child/adult ratios as low as possible.

Once the children are used to the routines and more secure in their connections to school, we as educators may use our ingenuity and expertise in child development to embed learning within routines and the children's play. This practice allows the children to develop and reinforce skills that are common across all settings rather than being specific to home or school. Then breathe and listen. The children will begin to communicate their strengths and interests. Observe and listen. The children's ideas will begin to flow. Record their ideas with them. Share the ideas as a group and listen.

Projects will begin to emerge. Go ahead; rediscover the joy in wondering along with the children. Take it further by accessing the community, colleagues, and team members to share their related strengths as you pursue the interests of the children.

The project approach is an integral piece of the strengths-based process because it listens to children's interests and empowers them to use their interests and other strengths as expressions of their capacity to develop further. Through the project approach process, young children learn and put to use their rote memory skills of identifying and naming colors, shapes, letters, numbers, nouns, verbs, and other attributes. More notably, the project approach naturally offers opportunities for the children to develop and employ higher-level skills such as planning, problem-solving, negotiating, collaborating, and co-constructing, as well as creativity and ingenuity. To Trent's special education teacher who came to work on a specific and isolated skill set with him, his fanciful, wooden-bead garden may have appeared to be unrelated and obscure. Yet when we dissect interactions such as Trent's for the strengths and skills children have used during them, we are able to gather data on the children's propensity for creativity and ingenuity.

By honoring the children's ideas with attention, respect, and resources, educators affirm them as great ideas. Educators promote the thinking through of the children's great ideas by guiding them through the process from the planning to the execution. We grow as professionals when we shift from thinking of teaching as filling the vessel to allowing the children to reach new levels as we facilitate their learning. By respectfully listening to and guiding the children's great ideas through the higher-level thinking processes of communicating, negotiating, planning, problem-solving, constructing materials, and creating story lines of play as they engage with peers, we permit the children to develop skills far beyond rote learning. As educators, we may take the children's development further by negotiating with the children about which of their ideas to follow as the next learning venue, which the class then explores.

As educators, when we follow a strengths-based project approach, we share in the gathering and creation of materials with the children and those in the greater educational community. As the children envision their great ideas, they will need access to an array of materials. Having the children communicate about the type of materials they need allows educators to facilitate the gathering process. By offering an assortment of common, child-friendly materials, the children begin to see potential for project work in materials they find at home, Grandma's house, religious classes, the recycle bin, and so forth. We suggest promoting this further by including natural materials in the collections. Often schools will follow a "leave nature in nature" rule to avoid having every child bring in handpicked weeds or rocks to the teacher every day. (These acts speak clearly to the draw that children have to nature.) Another approach may be to reinforce that we want to leave nature undisturbed, but may bring in a set amount to observe and use in the class.

Debbie has added narrow sections of tree limbs to her block area. The sections vary in height, width, and length sizes. Denise has an antique shadow box in her room. She also has a basket with a piece of cardboard hanging from its side, which has been cut to the size of the largest shadow box compartment. The children bring the basket on hikes and may each collect one favorite item that measures smaller than the cardboard piece. This guarantees that each natural treasure will fit within the shadow box compartments back in the class. Permitting the children to create or play with natural materials spurs such creation and play across all settings where children encounter nature. As you have begun to imagine, these creations and the play naturally lend themselves to developing concepts of size attributes, using unconventional units of measurement, one-to-one correspondence, and more.

Starting with children's strengths brings the joys of exploration and discovery to the early childhood setting for young children and the young-at-heart educators.

Glossary

Annual Review—On an annual basis, children's IEPs are reviewed, which includes a present level of performance that leads to goals for the upcoming year.

Children with Special Rights—A term coined from the schools in Reggio Emilia, the term *Child with Special Needs* has evolved to the *Child with Special Rights*. This term infers not only the right to a free and appropriate education, but also refers to the child's right to be respected as a competent researcher and communicator when given the resources and respect to investigate the world and communicate through his or her strongest language.

Co-constructive Learning—A process of learning in which teachers and students are making decisions about topics of interest and researching those topics together. Teachers use student's prior knowledge, ideas, and interests to engage the learning process and create new learning opportunities for all involved.

Collaborate—In this book the term *collaborate* or *collaborative learning* refers to a team approach to teaching and learning that involves generating ideas, activities, strategies, and problem-solving with all involved in a child's learning experience. This collaboration includes: the child, the teacher, the instructional assistants, the family, the therapists, and anyone else who is part of the child's learning experience.

Echolalia—The involuntary repetition of words or phrases spoken by others that lacks function speech, often a symptom of autism.

Eligibility Meeting—A meeting that involves a team consisting of parents, assessors such as special education teachers, therapists, and administrative representatives of the schools, in which evidence is provided as to the current level of development or performance of a child and whether the child is eligible for special education services.

Emotional Regulation—The ability to properly regulate one's emotions, which are influenced by the perception of sensations around us, the ability to think through emotions in a cognitive manner, filter out physiological responses (such as heart rate, breathing rate, etc.), and the ability to self-calm. Emotional regulation is a developmental process that requires initial co-regulation with caregivers with infants and progresses as children learn to self-calm. The development of emotional regulation can be disrupted through various issues such as a child's own sensory system, external issues, environmental problems, and cognitive delays, as well as other factors.

Facilitate Learning—The approach to teaching that involves providing students with the necessary resources and supports to learn according to their own style. In this approach the teacher views the learning process as an exploration by the student through which he or she gathers new information as opposed to the teacher imparting knowledge through lecturing or showing a child the answers.

Individualized Education Program (IEP)—This program includes the strengths and interests of the child and the present level of the child's performance, which then determines the goals for the child for the upcoming year. Once goals are established, any accommodations for the child as well as the special education services needed to aid in accomplishing those goals are decided.

IEP Meetings—Once a child has been found eligible for special education, a meeting is held to create an IEP. The IEP is formed through a team approach that includes the family (including the child if age-appropriate), the teacher(s), therapists, administrators, and other members that the school or family might feel appropriate, such as a parent advocate.

Picture Exchange Communication System (PEC)—An augmentative/alternative communication system that teaches children and adults with autism and other communication deficits to initiate communication.

Perseverative Behaviors—The tendency to continue or repeat a behavior or a vocalization over and over again.

Present Levels of Academic Achievement and Functional Performance (PLAAFP)—Present Level of Performance (PLP) is the portion of the child's IEP that details how the child's performance at that specific time. An accurate and complete PLP is essential for determining appropriate goals. Teachers, therapists, and parents contribute their observations on the student's performance level in academic and nonacademic areas, including the child's strengths and interests. Test scores are included as appropriate to further document the child's current level of ability.

Proprioceptive Sense—This refers to the sensory input and feedback that tell us about movement and body position. Its receptors are located within our muscles, joints, ligaments, tendons, and connective tissues.

Provocations—The specific materials or areas that teachers arrange for a center, a small group, or the whole class, which serve to promote experimentation, discovery, and learning in young children.

Scaffolding—The process in which others who are working with a child adjust the level of help provided in response to the child's level of performance in order to help the child achieve the next level of development.

Triennials—A child who has been qualified for special education is reassessed every 3 years to determine if he or she continues to be qualified to receive special education services.

Zone of Proximal Development (ZPD)—The zone of proximal development refers to the level of development that the child cannot reach by him- or herself but, given the support, or scaffolding, from an adult or a more capable peer, the child is able to develop those new skills or ideas.

Sample Parent Questionnaire

1. Who is _____? (Describe your child including information such as the child's personality, like, dislikes, favorite books or movies, etc., and place in your family.)

2. What are _____ strengths? (Including educational, social, motor [physical], etc.)

3. What are _____ interests?

4. What are _____ greatest challenges?

5. What supports are needed to help _____ reach his/her potential?

6. What are your dreams for _____?

7. What other information will help us as we look forward to working with your child for this year?

Multiple Intelligences Form

Howard Gardner has led thinking among educators about the many ways in which children can be "smart." Gardner's taxonomy has been very helpful in our efforts to use children's innate interests and strengths as a hood to learning. The following descriptions are not intended as way of "typing" children, but as a way of reaching a more comprehensive understanding of each child. Consider the descriptions below to begin theorizing about or describing your child's learning style.

Please circle all that apply to your child.

Intelligence	Preferences	Learns best by
Verbal-Linguistic Intelligence	Stories Writing Reading	Saying, hearing and seeing words
Logical/Mathematical Intelligence	Exploring patterns Figuring things out Working with numbers Experimenting Exploring relationships	Categorizing Classifying Working with patterns
Spatial Intelligence	Drawing, building, designing "Daydreaming" Looking at pictures	Visualizing Using the "mind's eye" Working with colors and pictures
Musical Intelligence	Singing, humming Listening to music Playing an instrument Moving to music	Rhythm and melody Music
Kinesthetic Intelligence	Moving Touching Talking	Processing knowledge through the body, touching, moving
Interpersonal Intelligence	Interacting with friends Talking with people Learning with others	Sharing & comparing Cooperating Interviewing
Intrapersonal Intelligence	Pursuing own interests Working alone	Working alone Individual projects Having own space Self-paced learning
Naturalist Intelligence	Being outdoors Classifying/sorting Interest in animals Collecting	Learning outside Having natural world brought indoors (plants, pets, natural collections)

Time Sampling: Areas of Interest

Observation of area played in at ___ minute intervals

Centers or Areas:

Date: _____
B= Block Area   D= Dramatic Play
A= Art Area   P= Puzzles
M= Manipulatives   L= Literacy (letters, books, stories, etc.)
(List area of interest and a short explanation of child's activity.)

Child's Name	1st Interval	2nd Interval	3rd Interval	4th Interval

Template for Skill Checklist

Fine Motor
U = Unskilled in this area
E = Emerging Skill
P = Proficient in this area

Child's Name	Scissors	Glue	Tape	Beading	Marker/Crayon Grip

Child Observed: Date:

Time Began: Time Ended:

Length of Interval: Context of Play:

Observation of Levels of Play and Social Interaction: A Time Sampling

Please see following page for detailed description of the levels of play.

Level of Play	Observation (1-minute observation, every 10 minutes)						
	1	2	3	4	5	6	7
1. Unoccupied							
2. Onlooker							
3. Solitary Play							
4. Parallel Play							
5. Associative Play							
6. Cooperative Play							
Comments:							

SIX CLASSIFICATIONS OF PLAY/SOCIAL INTERACTION

1. **Unoccupied Behavior**—The child is not engaged in any obvious play activity or social interaction, and will, instead, watch anything of interest or that might catch her attention at the time. When there is nothing to watch the child will play with his or her own body or move about from one place to another, follow the teacher, or stay in one spot looking around the room.

2. **Onlooker Behavior**—The child spends most of his or her time watching other children play. While the child may talk to, ask questions of, or offer suggestions to other children who are playing, he or she does not actually enter into play. The child will remain within speaking distance in order to hear and see what is going on, which indicates an interest in groups of children, unlike the unoccupied behavior, which only shows a shifting interest in what is going on at that moment.

3. **Solitary Play**—The child is involved in a play activity that is conducted independently of what anyone else is doing. The child plays with different materials and toys than those children around him or her, and makes no effort to get closer to or speak to them. The child in solitary play is entirely focused on his or her own activity and not influenced by those around him or her.

4. **Parallel Play**—The child in parallel play tends to play close to other children but is still independent of them in his or her own play. The child engages with toys and materials that are similar to those used by other children but is not influenced by others or their play. The child may also use those materials in a different manner than those around him or her. The child in parallel play plays alongside other children rather than with them.

5. **Associative Play**—In associative play the child plays with other children and there is a sharing of materials or equipment. The children may follow each other around and there may be attempts to control who plays in different groups. In associative play, however, there is no real division of labor or planned organization of play activities or children. Children may play similarly but not identically with one another. The child's individual desire in play is primary, rather than the interests of the group as a whole.

6. **Cooperative or Organized Supplementary Play**—In cooperative play, children play in a group that is organized around and established for a specific purpose— creating a product or a game or completing some kind of goal in play. There is a definite establishment of a group in which there are specific members forming that group. There is also some leadership within the group, with one or two of the children taking on the responsibility of directing the play. Organized play requires a division of labor, a taking on of different roles in order to complete the task or goal and the support of one child's effort by those of the others (Dodge, Colker, & Heroman, 2002).

Sample Activity Matrix for Objectives

WEEK OF:		
Name:	**Hannah**	**Crystal**
Arrival	Use simple fasteners with 1 assist	Follow routine directions with visual aids
Center	Draw a face with eyes, nose, hair, & a mouth Identify positional concepts: front/back; bottom/top; behind/in front of; & over/under Identify: circle, square, & triangle Demonstrate use of objects Take turns in simple games	Point to objects named Activate cause-and-effect toys Place circle and square on form board Play alongside peers
Snack	N/A	Use a straw with juice box Pick up finger food with pincer grasp
Circle	Sequence a 3-part story with one adult prompt Count to 5 in a rote manner Attend in circle for 10 minutes Name common body parts	Point to pictures in a book Imitate sounds
Lunch	Open simple containers Cut soft food w/ knife	Indicate food preference by choosing corresponding pictures Sign or gesture for "Help"
Outside	Play cooperative games with peers	Indicate choices through signs, visual aids, or pointing

WEEK OF:		
Name:	**Jake**	**Danielle**
Arrival	Take care of personal belongings with 1 prompt	Take care of personal belongings with 1 prompt
Center	Identify positional concepts: front/back; bottom/top Identify use of objects Identify same/different Identify circle square & triangle Identify colors: yellow, orange, & purple	Identify colors: blue, green, yellow, red, orange Identify square, rectangle, & triangle Identify familiar objects by their use Clean up toys & materials Toilet independently
Snack	Open simple containers	N/A
Circle	Participate in songs and finger plays Attend for 10-15 minutes in large group setting	Respect peers' personal space Attend for 10-15 minutes in large group setting Comply with adult directives
Lunch	Engage in conversation with peers and adults	Follow simple rules
Outside	Engage in turn-taking	Demonstrate caution, avoid common dangers

Activity Matrix designed by Penny George, 2005. Used with permission.

Symptoms of Sensory Processing Difficulties

TACTILE SYSTEM

The tactile system includes nerves under the skin's surface that send information to the brain. This information includes light touch, pain, temperature, and pressure. These sensations play an important role in how children perceive the world. Everyone has differences in the sensitivity to touch and pressure; however, children who are experiencing processing problems may indicate so in the following ways:

Hypersensitivity to Touch:

- Withdrawing when being touched
- Refusing to eat certain "textured" foods and/or to wear certain types of clothing
- Sensitive about having his/her hair or face washed,
- Avoids getting his/her hands dirty (i.e., glue, sand, mud, finger paint)
- May use just fingertips rather than whole hands to manipulate objects
- May be sensitive about textures of foods and/or not tolerate new foods
- May avoid close contact such as hugs
- May overreact to getting bumped by others or falling down
- Sensitive to clothing texture, may want tags removed or will only wear certain types of fabrics

Hyposensitivity to Touch:

- Tends to touch things roughly, has a hard time not touching others, may even hit him/herself or others
- Initiates affection frequently (i.e., gives and requests deep hugs)
- Does not seem to be aware of messiness on face or hands, may need to be reminded often to "wipe your face"
- May want to chew on crunchy items, puts things in his/her mouth, or will drink fluids in excess, may "overstuff" when eating
- Does not seem to notice when falling down or getting bumped

- Enjoys "falling" into bean bags, beds, chairs, etc.
- Pinches or bites himself or others, pushes and bumps into objects or people intentionally
- Is very attracted to playing with sensory materials, such as water, sand, rice, mud, etc.

VESTIBULAR SYSTEM

The vestibular system refers to structures within the inner ear that detect movement and changes in the position of the head and affect our sense of balance. Dysfunction within this system may manifest itself in two different ways.

Hypersensitivity to Vestibular Stimulation:

- Fearful reactions to ordinary movement activities (e.g., swings, slides, ramps, inclines)
- A hesitancy to walk or crawl on uneven surfaces
- May be delayed in learning to walk
- May have difficulty in learning to climb or descend stairs
- A tendency to appear clumsy

Hyposensitivity to Vestibular Stimulation:

- Actively seeks intense movement
  - » Spinning
  - » Swinging
  - » Jumping
- Enjoys rocking
- Wants to be picked up and held upside-down

THE PROPRIOCEPTIVE SYSTEM

The proprioceptive system involves the muscles, joints, and tendons that provide a person with a subconscious awareness of body position. The proprioceptive system provides signals that let us know what how much pressure it takes to hold a glass, where the glass is in relation to our mouth as we take a drink and how we might need to adjust our body as we complete that task.

Some Signs of Proprioceptive Dysfunction Are:

- Clumsiness
- A tendency to fall
- A lack of awareness of body position in space
- Minimal crawling when young
- Difficulty manipulating small objects (buttons, snaps)

- Avoidance of "fine motor" toys such as beading
- Eating in a "sloppy" manner
- May resist new motor movement activities
- Tends to break toys, crayons, etc. because of rough handling of materials
- Tends to "bump" into other people, walls, doorways, etc.

References

Angell, M. E., Stoner, J. B., & Fulk, B. M. (2010, January/February). Advice from adults with physical disabilities on fostering self-determination during the school years. *Teaching Exceptional Children, 42*(3), 64–75.

Arter, J., & Spandel, V. (1991). *Using portfolios of student work in instruction and assessment.* Portland, OR: Northwest Regional Educational Laboratory.

Block, M., & Chandler, B. E. (2005, January). Understanding the challenge. *OT Practice, 10*(1), CE-1–CE-8.

Booth, C. (1997). The fiber project: One teacher's adventure toward emergent curriculum. *Young Children, 52*(5), 79–85.

Branson, D. M., & Bingham, A. (2009, June). Using interagency collaboration to support family-centered transition practices. *Young Exceptional Children, 12*(3), 15–31.

Brazelton, B. (1992). *Touchpoints: The essential reference—Your child's emotional and behavioral development.* Reading, MA: Perseus Books.

Bricker, D. (2002). *AEPS: Assessment, evaluation, and programming system for infants and children.* Baltimore, MD: Paul H. Brookes.

Bricker, D., Clifford, J., Yovanaoff, P., Pretti-Frontzcak, K., Waddell, M., Allen, D., & Hoselton, R. (2008, December). Eligibility self-determination using a curriculum-based assessment: A further examination. *Journal of Early Intervention, 31*(1), 3–21.

Broer, S., Edelman, S. W., & Giangreco, M. F. (2001). Respect, appreciation, and acknowledgement of paraprofessionals who support students with disabilities. *Exceptional Children, 67*(4), 485–497.

Campbell, S. B., Shaw, D. S., & Gilliom, M. (2000). Early externalizing behavior problems: Toddlers and preschoolers at risk for later maladjustment. *Development and Psychopathology, 12*(3), 467–488.

Capizzi, A. M. (2008). From assessment to annual goal: Engaging a decision-making process in writing measurable IEPs. *Teaching Exceptional Children, 41*(1), 18–35.

Carnahan, C. R., Williamson, P., Clarke, L., & Sorensen, R. (2009, May/June). A systematic approach for supporting paraeducators in educational settings: A guide for teachers. *Teaching Exceptional Children, 41*(5), 34–43.

Carter, M., Cividanes, W., Curtis, D., & Lebo, D. (2010). Becoming a reflective teacher. *Teaching Young Children/Preschool, 3*(4), 18–20.

Casey, A. M., & McWilliam, R. A. (2007). The STARE: The Scale for Teachers' Assessment of Routines Engagement. *Young Exceptional Children, 11*(1), 2–15.

Casey, A. M. & McWilliam, R. A. (2005). Where is everybody? Organizing adults to promote child engagement. *Young Exceptional Children, 8*(2), 2–10.

Cheatham, G. A., & Ostrosky, M. M. (2009). Listening for details of talk: Early childhood parent-teacher conference communication facilitators. *Young Exceptional Children, 13*(1), 36–49.

DiCarlo, C. F., & Vagianos, L. (2009, September). Using child preferences to increase play across interest centers in inclusive early childhood classrooms. *Young Exceptional Children, 12*(4), 31–39.

Dodge, D. T. Colker, L. J. & Heroman, C. (2002).*The creative curriculum for preschool.* Washington, DC: Teaching Strategies.

Edwards, C., Gandini, L., & Forman, G. (1993). *The hundred languages of children: The Reggio Emilia approach to early childhood education.* Norwood, NJ: Ablex.

Epps, S., & Jackson, B. J. (2000). *Empowered families, successful children.* Washington, DC: American Psychological Association.

Fitzgerald, K. L., & Craig-Unkefer, L. (2008, September). Promoting humor with prekindergarten children with and without language impairments in classroom settings. *Young Exceptional Children, 11*(4), 13–25.

Ganz, J. B., & Flores, M. M. (2010). Supporting the play of preschoolers with autism spectrum disorders: Implementation of visual scripts. *Young Exceptional Children, 13*(2), 58–70.

Gardner, H. (1993). *Multiple intelligences.* New York: Basic Books.

Gartrell, D. (2004). *The power of guidance. Teaching social-emotional skills in early childhood classrooms.* Clinton Park, NY: Delmar Learning.

George, P. (2005) *Children's Learning Matrix.* Richmond, VA: Author.

Gestwicki, C. (1999). *Developmentally appropriate practice: Curriculum and development in early education* (2nd. ed.). Clinton Park, NY: Delmar Learning.

Gischlar, K. L., Hojnoski. R. L., & Missall, K. N. (2009, December). Improving child outcomes with data-based decision making: Interpreting and using data. *Young Exceptional Children, 13*(1), 2–18.

Grace, C. (1992). *The portfolio and its use: Developmentally appropriate assessment of young children.* ERIC Digest. (071); Eric Identifer ED351150. Retrieved March 31, 2011, from http://ericae.net/edo/ed351150.htm

Grace, C., Shores, E. F., & Brown, M. H. 1991. *The portfolio and its use: Developmentally appropriate assessment of young children.* Little Rock, AR: Southern Association on Children Under Six.

Gredler, M., & Shields, C. (2007*). Vygotsky's legacy: A foundation for research and practice.* New York: The Guilford Press.

Greenberg, M. T., Cicchetti, D., & Cummings, E. M. (1990). *Attachment in the preschool years.* Chicago: The University of Chicago Press.

Greenspan, S. I. (1997). *The growth of the mind.* Reading, MA: Perseus Books.

Greenspan, S. I., & Wieder, S. (1998). *The child with special needs.* Reading, MA: Perseus Books.

Harris, K., & Gleim, L. (2008) The light fantastic: Making learning visible for all children through the project approach. *Young Exceptional Children, 11*(3), 27–39.

Harte, H. A. (2009, Sept/Oct). What teachers can learn from mothers of children with autism. *Teaching Exceptional Children, 42*(1), 24–30.

Helm, J. H. (July, 2008). Got standards? Don't give up on engaged learning! *Young Children, 63*, 14-20. Retrieved from http://www.naeyc.org/files/yc/file/200807/BTJJudyHarrisHelm.pdf

Helm, J. H., & Beneke, S. (Eds.). (2003). *The power of projects: Meeting contemporary challenges in early childhood classrooms–Strategies and solutions.* New York: Teachers College Press.

Helm, J. H., Beneke, S., & Steinheimer, K. (2007). *Windows on learning: Documenting young children's work* (2nd. ed.). New York: Teachers College Press.

Hollingsworth, H. L., Able Boone, H., & Crais, E. R. (2009, December). Individualized inclusion plans at work in early childhood classrooms. *Young Exceptional Children, 13*(1), 19–35.

Jolivette, K., Stichter, J. P., & McCormick, K. M. (2002). Making choices—Improving behavior—Engaging in learning. *Teaching Exceptional Children, 34*(3), 24–29.

Jones, B. F., Valdez, G., Nowakowski, J., & Rasmussen, C. (1994). *Designing learning and technology for educational reform*. Oak Brook, IL: North Cental Regional Educational Laboratory.

Jung, L. A. (2007, March/April). Writing SMART objectives and strategies that fit the ROUTINE. *Teaching Exceptional Children, 39*(4), 54–58.

Jung, L. A., Gomez, C., Baird, S. M., & Keramidas, C. G. (2008). Designing intervention plans: Bridging the gap between Individualized Education Programs and implementation. *Teaching Exceptional Children, 41* (1), 26–33.

Kemmis, B. L. & Dunn, W. (1996, October). Collaborative consultation: The efficacy of remedial and compensatory interventions in school contexts. *The American Journal of Occupational Therapy, 50*(9), 709–71.

Koenig, K. P., Bleiweiss, J., Brennan, S., Cohen, S., & Siegel, D. E. (2009, September/October). The ASD Nest Program: A model for inclusive public education for students with autism spectrum disorders. *Teaching Exceptional Children, 42*(1), 6–13.

Koplow, L. (2002) *Creating schools that heal*. New York: Teachers College Press.

Koplow, L. (Ed.). (2007). *Unsmiling faces* (2nd ed.). New York: Teachers College Press.

Kranowitz, C. S. (1998). *The out-of-sync child: Recognizing and coping with sensory integration dysfunction*. New York, NY: Berkley Publishing Group.

Linder, T. W. (1999). *Read, play, and learn! Storybook activities for young children*. Baltimore: Paul H. Brookes.

Lytle, R., & Todd, T. (2009, March/April). Stress and the student with autism spectrum disorders: Strategies for stress reduction and enhanced learning. *Teaching Exceptional Children, 41*(4), 36–42.

Marvin, R., Cooper, G., Hoffman, K., & Powell, B. (2002, April). The circle of security project: Attachment-based intervention with caregiver–pre-school child dyads. *Attachment & Human Development, 4*(1), 107–124.

Mastrangelo, S. (2009). Harnessing the power of play opportunities for children with autism spectrum disorders. *Teaching Exceptional Children, 42*(1), 34–44.

Meins, E., Fernyhough, C., Wainwright, R., Das Gupta, M., Fradley, E., & Tuckey, M. (2002, November/December). Maternal mind-mindedness and attachment security as predictors of theory of mind understanding. *Child Development, 73*(6), 1715–1726.

Mitchell, D. B., & Hauser-Cram, P. (2009, December). Early predictors of behavior problems: Two years after early intervention. *Journal of Early Intervention, 32*(1), 3–16.

Morrison, R. (1999). Picture this! Using portfolios to facilitate the inclusion of children in preschool settings. *Early Childhood Education Journal, 27*(1), 45–48.

National Association for the Education of Young Children. (2009). Developmentally appropriate practice in early childhood programs serving children from birth through 8. Retrieved 3/23/11 from www.naeyc.org/about/position/dap4.asp

National Research Council Institute of Medicine. (2000). *From neurons to neighborhoods*. Washington, DC: National Academy Press.

Odom, S. L. (2000). Preschool inclusion: What we know and where we go from here. *Topics in Early Childhood Special Education, 20*(1), 20–27.

Olson, J., Murphy, C. L., & Olson, P. D. (1999, May). Readying parents and teachers for the inclusion of children with disabilities: A step-by-step process. *Young Children, 54*(3), 18–22.

Osborne, L. A., & Reed, P. (2009). The relationship between parenting stress and behavior problems of children with autistic spectrum disorders. *Exceptional Children, 76*(1), 54–73.

Paley, V. (1986). On listening to what the children say. *Harvard Educational Review, 56*(2), 122–132.

Paley, V. (1991). *The boy who would be a helicopter*. Cambridge, MA: Harvard University Press.

Parish, S. L., Rose, R. A., & Andrews, M. E. (2010). TANF's impact on low-income mothers raising children with disabilities. *Exceptional Children, 76*(2), 234–253.

Parish, S. L., Rose, R. A, Grinstein-Weiss, M., Richman, E. L., & Andrews, M. E. (2008). Material hardship in U.S. families raising children with disabilities. *Exceptional Children, 75*(1), 71–92.

Pelco, L. E., & Reed-Victor, E. (2003). Understand and supporting differences in child temperament. *Young Exceptional Children, 6*(3), 2–11.

Polce-Lynch, M. (2002). *Boy talk*. Oakland, CA: New Harbinger.

Pretti-Frontczak, K., & Bricker, D. (2004). *An activity-based approach to early intervention* (3rd ed.). Baltimore, MD: Paul H. Brookes.

Reebye, P., & Stalker, A. (2008) *Understanding regulation disorders of sensory processing in children*. London and Philadelphia: Jessica Kingsley Publishers.

Sandall, S., Hemmeter, M. L., Smith, B. J., & McLean, M. E. (2005). *DEC recommended practices*. Longmont, CO: Sopris West Educational Services.

Scholtes, P. R., Joiner, B. L., & Streibel, B. J. (2003). *The team handbook*. Madison, WI: Oriel.

Shannon, P. (2004, April). Barriers to family-centered services for infants and toddlers with developmental delays. *Social Work, 49*(2), 301–307.

Siegel, D. J. (1999). *The developing mind*. New York: The Guilford Press.

Sussna, A. G. (2000). A quest to ban cute—And make learning truly challenging. *Dimensions of Early Childhood, 28*(2), 3–7.

Trent-Stainbrook, A., Kaiser, A. P., & Frey, J. R. (2007, Summer). Older siblings' use of responsive interaction strategies and effects on their younger siblings with Down Syndrome. *Journal of Early Intervention, 29*(4), 273–286

Turnbull, A.P., Turnbull, H. R., Erwin, E., & Soodak, L. (2006). *Families, professionals, and exceptionality. (Positive outcomes through partnership and trust.)* Upper Saddle River, NJ: Pearson Merrill

Vakil, S., Freeman, R., & Swim, T. J. (2003). The Reggio Emilia approach and inclusive early childhood programs. *Early Childhood Education Journal, 30*(3), 187–192.

Vygotsky, L. S. (1978). *Mind in society: The development of higher psychological processes*. Cambridge, MA: Harvard University Press.

Winsler, A., Diaz, R. M., Atencio, D. J., McCarthy, E. M., & Chabay, L. A. (2000). Verbal self-regulation over time in children at risk for attention and behavior problems. *Journal of Child Psychology and Psychiatry, 41*(7), 875–886.

Xu, Y. (2008, December).Developing meaningful IFSP outcomes through a family-centered approach using the double ABCX model. *Young Exceptional Children, 12*(1), 2–19.

Index

Note: Page numbers followed by f and t indicate presence of figures and tables respectively.

Strengths-based narrative, example of, 129–130
Strengths-based PLAAFP, example of, 127–128
Superheros project, lesson planning and, 117–119, 118f–119f
    sample plans, 120t–122t
Sussna, A. G., 45, 60, 82, 83, 105
Swim, T. J., 55, 82, 130
Systematic observation, checklist for, 48, 146–147

Tactile system, 150–151
Teacher-directed curriculum, 99
Teacher-directed lessons, risks in, 85–86
Teacher-initiated project, 112–113
    sample lesson plans, 114t–116t
Teacher/Teaching
    collaborative, 86–87, 94, 112, 135
    emotional connection to, 11–12
    learning activities and, 1–2
Theme-based curriculum
    combining with emergent curriculum, 107–109
    vs. emergent curriculum, 104–106, 105f
Themes
    nature-related, dramatic play and, 54
    planning, for project-based learning, 44–45
Therapists, collaboration with, 51
"The Three Little Pigs," combined theme-based and emergent curricula example, 108–109
Time
    for identifying learning strengths, 24
    for observation, 45–46
Time-sampling observation chart, 46, 144
Todd, T., 79
Touch
    hypersensitivity to, 150
    hyposensitivity to, 150–151
Touchpoints (Brazelton), 10
Transdisciplinary team, 29–30
    communication strategies, 33–35
    data collection and documentation by, 130
    strength-based approaches to creating, 126–130
    trust practices in, 30–33

Traveling notebooks, 34
Trent-Stainbrook, A., 125
Trienniels, 125, 140
Trust
    defined, 30
    practices within transdisciplinary team, 30–33
Tuckey, M., 73
Turnbull, A. P., 28, 30, 124
Turnbull, H. R., 28, 30, 124

Understanding Regulation Disorders of Sensory Processing in Children (Reebye & Stalker), 7
Unit approach. *See* Project-based learning
Unoccupied behavior, 147
    time sampling chart for, 146

Vagianos, L., 46, 47, 74, 103, 105, 106, 109, 110
Vakil, S., 55, 82, 130
Valdez, G., 81
Verbal communication, 9
Vestibular stimulation
    hypersensitivity to, 151
    hyposensitivity to, 151
Vestibular system, 151
Volunteers, 51–52
Vygotsky, L. S., 87

Waddell, M., 124, 125
Wainwright, R., 73
Wieder, S., 10, 11, 73, 77
Williamson, P., 51
Winsler, A., 70, 73, 96

Xu, Y., 30

Yovanaoff, P., 124, 125

Zone of proximal development (ZPD), 87, 140
    scaffolding and (student vignettes), 87–93, 88f, 90f, 93f

About the Authors

Debbie C. Lickey, M.Ed., holds certifications in K–3 and Early Childhood Special Education. Debbie has been working in the early childhood field for the last 25 years as a teacher, program director, and consultant. Debbie works for the Partnership for People with Disabilities at Virginia Commonwealth University as a project coordinator to enhance community college early childhood programs' inclusion of content about working with young children who have disabilities. Debbie currently lives in Richmond, Virginia, with her husband, three children, and three dogs.

Denise J. Powers, M.Ed., holds certifications in Elementary and Special Education, birth–age 21. Denise has taught in elementary and early childhood special education settings for the past 25 years. Denise is the early childhood specialist in The Circle Preschool Program, a therapeutic program of Greater Richmond Stop Child Abuse Now (SCAN), for young children and their caregivers. Denise lives in Richmond, Virginia, with her husband, three daughters, and two dogs.

Debbie and Denise both studied the early childhood programs in Reggio Emilia, Italy. The experience of learning about the hundred languages of children reinforced their commitment to discovering each child's strengths as their basis for teaching young children.